T0039007

"Sarah Westfall's words in *The Way of Belonging* are poetic and pierce the heart. She reminds us that true belonging and connection cannot be manufactured, checked off a list, faked, or forced. True belonging and connection emerge from finding home with God and others. Home transcends walls, roofs, and lines; it's the place where unconditional love, acceptance, and worthiness are found."
Terence Lester, founder of Love Beyond Walls and author of *All God's Children*

"Maybe you, like me, are homesick for Eden. And maybe your longing to belong is an invitation to a better story, one in which your heartache is honored, your questions are held, and your deepest desires are given space to be spoken. Sarah Westfall's exquisite book reawakened my own heart, opening me to currents streaming within that I'd been ignoring of late. It will thaw your heart too, awakening a hunger and a thirst for the Edenic inheritance of belonging tucked deep within your heart."
Chuck DeGroat, author of *When Narcissism Comes to Church* and professor of pastoral care at Western Theological Seminary

"In this kind and relatable debut work, Sarah Westfall offers a spiritually formative resource for anyone who questions their place with people, with God, or with themselves. While reading *The Way of Belonging*, I found myself nodding my head and sighing with relief. I'm grateful for this honest book."
Emily P. Freeman, author of *The Next Right Thing* and *How to Walk into a Room*

"With tender wisdom, warmth, and depth, Sarah E. Westfall invites us to examine our communal desire for belonging and journey with her into a lifelong practice of welcome. Sarah generously shares her own story and struggle while extending a hand of hope and hard-earned insight. I found my own wrestling alongside the stories she shared and found hope and a way forward for all of us who have wandered and searched for belonging and come up short. *The Way of Belonging* is a book for our time and for all time—it is a gentle guide and a wise companion."
Tasha Jun, author of *Tell Me the Dream Again*

"When Sarah Westfall writes, I read. When Sarah speaks, I listen. Offering captivating narrative, scriptural wisdom, and a practical guide, *The Way of Belonging* will challenge long-held beliefs about belonging and offer a more life-giving approach to relationships as we consider belonging as a welcome we carry with us. Belonging is not something we passively hope for but rather a gift we are empowered to offer others when we absorb the reality of God's wide welcome of us. I feel excited about what might be possible in our hearts, relationships, and communities if we have the courage to practice what is written in this important book."
Nicole Zasowski, marriage and family therapist and author of *What If It's Wonderful?*

"Belonging can be a fraught concept—both essential as we live into the reality of our belovedness and yet complex for many of us. In *The Way of Belonging*, Sarah Westfall has masterfully woven together a picture of our need to become our God-given selves while balancing it with the yearning we have to matter in the hearts and lives of others. I'm so grateful for this beautiful book."

Aundi Kolber, licensed professional counselor and author of *Try Softer*

"In *The Way of Belonging*, Sarah Westfall makes room for all of us at the table, no matter who we are or where we come from. With eyes open to the empathy that builds for other people in suffering, we're invited to find our truest sense of belonging in God's love. Instead of working hard to fit in, we can exhale and move in to a fuller version of who we were made to be."

Sara Billups, author of *Orphaned Believers: How a Generation of Christian Exiles Can Find the Way Home* and *Nervous Systems*

"The epidemic of loneliness in our country is a real thing, and in her gentle and engaging fashion, Sarah offers the antidote: belonging. While so many in our world are concerned with self-preservation, this book encourages us to see the isolated among us and to extend a hand of love. Her words are a beautiful invitation into a different way of being."

Shawn Smucker, author of *The Day the Angels Fell*

THE WAY OF BELONGING

Reimagining Who We Are and How We Relate

SARAH E. WESTFALL

Foreword by Lore Ferguson Wilbert

An imprint of InterVarsity Press
Downers Grove, Illinois

InterVarsity Press
P.O. Box 1400 | Downers Grove, IL 60515-1426
ivpress.com | email@ivpress.com

©2024 by Sarah E. Westfall

All rights reserved. No part of this book may be reproduced in any form without written permission from InterVarsity Press.

InterVarsity Press® is the publishing division of InterVarsity Christian Fellowship/USA®. For more information, visit intervarsity.org.

Scripture quotations, unless otherwise noted, have been taken from the Christian Standard Bible®, Copyright © 2017 by Holman Bible Publishers. Used by permission. Christian Standard Bible® and CSB® are federally registered trademarks of Holman Bible Publishers.

While any stories in this book are true, some names and identifying information may have been changed to protect the privacy of individuals.

Published in association with The Bindery Agency, www.TheBinderyAgency.com.

The publisher cannot verify the accuracy or functionality of website URLs used in this book beyond the date of publication.

Cover design: David Fassett
Interior design: Daniel van Loon
Images: © oxygen / Moment via Getty Images; Getty Images Plus: © ElenaMichaylova / iStock, © prezent / iStock

ISBN 978-1-5140-0853-9 (print) | ISBN 978-1-5140-0854-6 (digital)

Printed in the United States of America ∞

Library of Congress Cataloging-in-Publication Data
Names: Westfall, Sarah Elizabeth, 1983- author.
Title: The way of belonging : reimagining who we are and how we relate / Sarah E. Westfall.
Description: Downers Grove, IL : IVP, [2024] | Includes bibliographical references.
Identifiers: LCCN 2023055956 (print) | LCCN 2023055957 (ebook) | ISBN 9781514008539 (print) | ISBN 9781514008546 (digital)
Subjects: LCSH: God–Love. | Belonging (Social psychology)–Religious aspects Christianity. | Identity (Psychology)–Religious aspects Christianity. | BISAC: RELIGION / Christian Living / Family & Relationships | SELF-HELP / Personal Growth / Happiness
Classification: LCC BT140 .W48 2024 (print) | LCC BT140 (ebook) | DDC 231.7–dc23/eng/20240125
LC record available at https://lccn.loc.gov/2023055956
LC ebook record available at https://lccn.loc.gov/2023055957

30 29 28 27 26 25 24 | 12 11 10 9 8 7 6 5 4 3 2 1

To Ben,

for the many miles we have walked together

and all that are yet to come.

CONTENTS

FOREWORD

LORE FERGUSON WILBERT

The psychiatrist Curt Thompson once wrote, "We are all born into the world looking for someone looking for us." If that is true, I sense most of us are still looking in one way or another. No earthly human, no organized institution, no group or family offers what we all long for in one way or another: complete, total, and more than anything, *unconditional* belonging.

Our belonging is contingent on our behavior or our identity or our beliefs or our ability to bear with differences. It seems contingent on whether we will go along to get along or if we view ourselves as a black sheep, content to stand apart. Our belonging is dependent on the ways we dress or don't dress, the foods we eat, the medicine we accept as good or bad, the doctors we choose, the church we attend, the friends we want, and the friends we definitely don't want. There is almost nothing in our lives that isn't touched by a sense of belonging or unbelonging. We read the books our groups read and hate the books other groups love. We watch the news that makes us feel safe and comforted, seen and valued, and we despise the news that does the same for others. We seek belonging in marriage, in children, in our parents, in our siblings, friends, pastors, leaders, neighbors, the mothers of other children, and the coworkers we work among.

And yet, amid this life of searching for belonging, most of us feel, even just on the margins of our souls, a sense of something missing. Always missing. A sense that somewhere along the way we took the wrong fork in the road or we missed our moment or someone else stole what was ours or somehow, someway, something went wrong and we will always be looking for those who are *not* looking for us too.

In this book, Sarah Westfall travels the roads of belonging, all the forks where the way of belonging may be found or has been lost. She illuminates her own stories of marginalization or being marginalized herself. She writes with candid care about the ways that we all face exclusion or ousting from others, and sometimes even from our own selves.

Sarah has been there before, and she's learned (and confesses she's still learning) the way through. This beautiful book can be like a companion for your own journey of belonging: a friend on the path with you, an arm linked with yours, a face that is looking for you to belong too. I hope you find in it a better belonging than you could have imagined.

Part I

WHO WE ARE

To surrender to Divine love is to find our soul's home—
the place and identity for which we
yearn in every cell of our being.

DAVID G. BENNER

We love because he first loved us.

1 JOHN 4:19

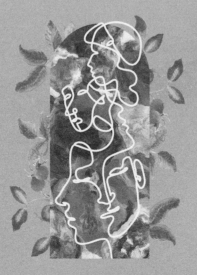

1

OUT OF PLACE

| I was born homesick. Maybe we all were. |

ANDREW PETERSON

I could see her out the corner of my eye. A woman from church who I did not know well lingered just off stage, clutching a notebook to her chest. She was clearly waiting for me, but I paused to give myself a moment. Tiredness had settled deep in my body, and my introverted tendencies were in full force. All I wanted was to be home in my sweatpants, but I knew I could not slip silently out the back door. At a conference I helped plan. About community. (Listen, the irony was not lost on me.)

I stepped off stage, and the woman inched closer.

Her face was familiar from passing each other on Sunday mornings, but we had never been formally introduced. She extended her hand, "Hi. I'm Jolene. I'm the one who asked the question about doing all the right things . . ."

A knot formed at the base of my stomach. I knew exactly what question she meant. During the last session of the conference, we had opened the floor for attendees to submit questions anonymously. Many submissions were expected: What opportunities does the church have for connection? What if I cannot attend a small group? You get the picture. But one question left me and the other speakers feeling like raccoons, wide eyes caught in stage lights with nowhere to run. In the moment, I had done my best to empathize with the struggle, but the truth was that I did not have an answer, at least not one that satisfied my soul. And with Jolene standing in front of me, it appeared the response had not satisfied her either.

We stood there, and Jolene softly repeated her question, "I have done all the things you guys talked about—showing up, inviting people over." Her voice wavered. "So why do I still feel like I don't belong?"

A moment of silence passed. Then another. And another. Part of me wanted to throw a blanket of "Oh, well just keep doing what you're doing . . ." over her pain so we could both go home, but as I stood there, my gut turning and twisting, I realized I had no idea what to tell her. Outside the regular community mantras of "be vulnerable, show up, be intentional," I did not know how to soothe her ache. I offered to meet her for coffee, but even as the words came out, the response seemed cheap in relation to the question with which she was entrusting me. Coffee and communion are far from the same.

How desperately I wanted to have a neat and tidy answer for her (and if I was being especially transparent, a neat and tidy answer for myself), but I knew Jolene was right. Belonging cannot be manufactured. It is not an idyllic destination "out there" waiting for us to arrive or a recipe we can cobble together in our kitchens (although a kitchen often seems a more likely place to find it than the round tables and hard chairs at church). There is no secret formula or five-step program that guarantees the connection we crave. We can do all the right things and still feel so dreadfully out of place.

I know this reality well, because despite all I have learned, practiced, and even taught about cultivating connection at church, on college campuses, and in our home, I am the one who often feels more outside than in.

I am the one who makes dinner plans but considers faking a fever right up until the moment I have to leave.

. I am the one who cringes when conversation stalls at small talk.

I am the one who walks into a room and makes my way to the food, just to have something to do with my hands.

More often than not, the thing that gets me out of bed and occupies most of my thoughts and conversations is also the thing that tucks me into bed at night full of questions. And while I could do without the perpetual self-doubt, I am exceedingly grateful for those questions, because I know I am not the only one asking them.

I am not the only one who wants more than surface relationships but struggles to know how much to share.

I am not the only one who wants to show up fully myself but often shrinks back in fear.

I am not the only one who has felt the sting of loneliness and wondered, *What does it really look like to belong?*

That day, Jolene and I said an awkward and inadequate goodbye. We never did meet for coffee, a regret that still causes twinges of guilt from time to time. But as I walked away, I knew I needed a better answer to the question we were both asking, because if belonging is not finding the right place or the right people, then what is it?

Back to the Beginning

For as long as I can remember, belonging is a desire I have carried. Some people are born with birthmarks or unusually loud laughs, but I was born with a want for connection wedged into the deepest parts of my body. As a child, I pursued connection with curiosity and nothing less. Unhindered by expectations, the yearning flowed freely as I ran across the backyard, over the short fence, to ask whether my friend Emily could come out to play. I did not wonder whether Emily wanted to come over, what we would talk about, or how my disheveled hair cascaded wildly down my back. I had not yet learned how fragile relationships could be or the ways we tend to lose ourselves trying to fit in. I had not yet felt the sting of being on the outside. All I had was unfettered joy as I ran barefoot across the grass.

I often wonder if that's what Adam and Eve experienced in the Garden. Prior to experiencing the pain of separation, was belonging simply part of their daily existence, as natural as the air that moved in and out of their newly formed lungs? Without shame in nearness or nakedness, did they run through the grass with arms extended toward God and each other? At night, as wind whistled through the trees and the rivers sang their lullabies, did man and woman close their eyes without fear or hesitation, knowing they were already home?

Even now as I imagine that kind of communion, I take a deep breath, a familiar wanting rising in my chest. Perhaps we are all just trying to get back to where we started, back to the place where we did not hesitate to run across the yard and find a friend. My pulse quickens at the thought of such safety and unbridled pursuit. Such purity of presence. What might it be like to return to our beginnings?

From the moment we come into the world, we are reaching. Our infant lips and limbs search for our mothers, craving attachment of body and soul. Without shame, we make known our need for the warmth and nearness of another person, tipping back our heads with primal yells and letting tears fall freely until we are safe and soothed. No hesitation. No second-guessing. All we know is that we want to be held.

As children, we looked for friends on playgrounds or down the street, because the desire for connection did not fill us with shame but moved us toward each other. If you were lonely, you simply asked to join the closest game of tag or knocked on a neighbor's door or climbed onto a parent's lap. Just last week my husband took our four boys to the park and our youngest son came home sweaty and eyes alight with excitement about a boy he met named Michael. They had played together only five minutes, but it was enough to call Michael a friend.

It is as if God's words "it is not good . . . to be alone" are molded into our marrow, wrapped around who we are like a double helix—unseen but always with us (Genesis 2:18). Belonging is central to who we are and how we interact, and unfettered, this desire moves us toward one another. But somewhere between that first breath and adulthood, we stop being so bold and outspoken about our need for one another. We stop knocking on doors and crying out quite as often. We get hurt and insecure and pull back, convincing ourselves that independence and individuality are good substitutes. As a result, we learn to swallow our loneliness, busying ourselves before we taste its bitterness on our tongues. We choose distraction in all its forms rather than let ourselves imagine that maybe this desire to belong is not some aimless pursuit, some flighty insecurity, but the truest truth about ourselves. Because if we really stopped and paid attention, we would see that the desire for with-ness has always been a part of who we are.

Learning to Hide

Until I was eleven, we lived on a slow street in the middle of town, the kind of street where kids were always popping in and out of alleys on bikes or playing with Skip-Its up and down the sidewalks. Every backyard was an extension of the others, and we would run from house to house until the sun grew lazy and parents called us home. In the days leading up to my sixth birthday party, I invited every kid on our little city block to join us (and then some). The decision was generous on my part, no doubt. The problem was that I forgot to inform my parents of the expanded guest list.

The day of the party arrived—and so did the kids. In fact, so many kids kept showing up that Mom and Dad had to drag three picnic tables together end to end just to make room, and even then, the adults still stood. That day, I imagine Mom crossed her fingers and prayed that Jesus would multiply our homemade cake like he had the loaves and fishes.

I do not remember much about that party beyond our family's retelling and a few pictures, but I love that story. There's one photograph in particular where I'm in the middle of all those kids standing on the picnic table bench, hands thrown over my head, red Popsicle dripping down my fingers, with a wide smile across my face. I marvel at that little girl, the one who did not hesitate to overextend an invitation. I wonder at her sense of safety to bring so many to the birthday table, to gather without expectation. Belonging was simple then, and all were welcomed. A little flurry of promise runs through me at the idea of being so openhanded and free. But I also have to ask: What happened to that little girl? When did I make the switch from gathering people to grasping for recognition? When did I begin to feel more outside than in?

For most of us, somewhere between those days of knocking on neighbors' doors and full-fledged adulthood, friendship gets complicated. The prerequisites seem to morph from proximity to acceptance, and any inherent sense of belonging fades beneath the desire to fit in. We begin to hesitate before walking into a room or choose isolation instead of sending the invitation. For me, the subtle shift began in kindergarten, just months after that summer birthday, and while the change was not caused by one person or isolated event, we all have moments that tend to collect and resurface from time to time, giving us glimpses into how we lost our way.

We had just come in from recess, faces red and eager for a turn at the drinking fountain. Securing a spot near the front of the line, I stepped forward. The white porcelain pressed against my small fingers as I balanced on tiptoes to take a sip. Stray water droplets trickled down my chin, and I was careful to catch them, not wanting a single dribble to fall onto the dress I had carefully picked out that morning.

To this day, I cannot remember the exact dress. In my mind the fabric was a soft blue cotton with puffed sleeves, because as a kindergarten girl in the 1990s, puffed sleeves were everything (thank you, Anne of Green Gables). What I do recall was how that dress made me feel. My shoulders squared proudly as I walked the halls of my small school. I loved who I was in that dress, and I was keenly aware that I did not want to ruin the fabric with a few drops of water.

Wiping my chin with the back of my hand, I finished my time at the fountain and turned toward one of my closest friends, Olivia. A slight frown spread across her face as she looked back at me and said, "That dress makes you look fat." The sentence was declarative, as if she were simply restating what she had for lunch or that the sky was blue. But this fact was news to me.

As Olivia moved past to get her drink, my body slumped. Hurt welled in my chest, threatening to spill down the face I had just wiped clean. I arrived at school that day alive, free, and confident in the girl I saw in the mirror. Six words was all it took to replace that sense of security with the sinking feeling I did not fit in. Even my best dress was not good enough. My body was not good enough. I turned away before Olivia finished her drink and saw tears pooling in my eyes.

I do not blame Olivia. One comment did not diminish all the hours we spent playing Barbies or the summers spent floating in her parents' in-ground pool, the smell of lemon juice wafting from our hair while Mariah Carey serenaded us from the boombox. Olivia was a dear friend, a steadfast companion, and I am certain I too uttered my fair share of careless words over the years. Because that's what happens when you spend enough time with someone. Sooner or later, intended or not, our jagged edges rub up against each other.

Therapist Ryan Kuja once told me, "To be human is to know something of trauma." Seen or unseen, real or imagined, intentional or not, we collect wounds like paper cuts along the way. Some traumas leave slivers while others create gaping holes in our sense of connection. Differences morph into divisions, and instead of throwing our hands wide and running across the grass toward each other, we just start running. Like Adam and Eve after that first bite of fruit, we hide. We cover parts of ourselves from God and each other, too afraid to bare what is tender and too hurt to move toward healing.

And that's how our original belonging begins to fade. What began in the Garden becomes a distant memory as we bury loneliness beneath the belief *I am the one who is out of place. The odd one out. The one who can't quite get it. The one who is not wanted or the one who feels awkward entering the room.* We think we are the only ones alone on the sidewalk, watching through the window at a crowd who has it all figured out.

Shifting the Question

Not long ago, I picked up Henri Nouwen's *The Return of the Prodigal Son.* I had been thinking a lot about Jesus' parable of the lost son (from Luke 15), and I checked out Nouwen's book hoping it would lend a little insight. But Nouwen's story tilted everything. I had one of those experiences where it felt like the words had been written for me and me alone, as if gears once clunky, banging and clanking against one another, finally fell into place and began to move smoothly. He wrapped words around ideas that had long been swirling inside me.

I told my friend Carla the following night at dinner that *The Return of the Prodigal Son* did more than solidify my solidarity with the self-righteous older brother in Jesus' story (more on that to come). Nouwen helped me reframe the question I had long been asking, from "What does it look like to belong?" to "How can I be a place of welcome?" The shift altered my posture from *me* to *we*. Because instead of wondering how to fit in, I began to consider what it might look like if we could (in Nouwen's words) "be home" to one another.

The realization came like a fresh rush of freedom, as if someone had just opened a window and released a promise my soul had long been holding.

Belonging is not something to attain but someone to become.

It is not about finding the right place or the right people but about embracing our worth as God's beloved and then extending the welcome.

What I wish I could have told Jolene that day at the conference is that maybe we have been looking at belonging all wrong. Maybe the meaningful connection we seek is not "out there" waiting to be discovered. Maybe we do not need to bend ourselves into countless iterations or get sweaty in pursuit of some cosmic combination of perfect place and perfect people. Because belonging is already in us—part of who we have always been and who we are becoming. And maybe those very wounds we want to hide can help us find our way back to God and to each other.

2

ALL THINGS LOST

> Not everything that fades has been stolen.

JAMES K. A. SMITH

As I moved through elementary school into the upper grades, I wrapped my identity in achievement, and that little girl who gathered the neighborhood became little more than a memory. I collected labels such as "straight-A student," "class president," and "softball team captain" like patches sewn on a heavy backpack. Each label became a way to beautify the lack I carried inside like a secret.

I morphed from friend group to friend group like a chameleon, from the cheerleaders to the choir kids, from church youth group to the teens who wore Black Sabbath shirts and smoked out behind the Bob Evans where I worked evenings and weekends. I belonged everywhere and nowhere all at once.

Hiding has a way of creating distance, of keeping ourselves and others at arm's length. We wrap thick layers of protection across our shoulders, hoping to be something other than human people who hurt and who feel, but in the process we do more than bury the desire for communion. We bury ourselves.

We cover up who we really are, hoping who we appear to be will be welcomed. But belonging and acceptance are not the same.

By the time high school graduation rolled around, I had convinced all of us—maybe even myself—that I had performed my way into belonging. If you had been there, watching me give a class president speech beneath the fluorescent hum of the gymnasium lights, you would not have believed I felt out of place. In my pale blue robes, gold cords draped around my shoulders, I appeared confident and secure. But achievement is an easy anesthetic. Beneath the accolades was a girl who wondered whether she was wanted, not for what she produced or how she presented but for the person underneath it all. I was not a prodigal, and yet, I could not shake the sense of being lost.

More Than Good

Many of us are familiar with Jesus' story in Luke 15, a tale we often refer to as the parable of the prodigal son. We talk about this story as a narrative of a rebellious, squandering youth who came to the end of himself and had nowhere to turn but home. We hear of a father squinting his eyes at the horizon, joy overtaking him as he sees his youngest son in the distance. All of this is true, but what we so often overlook is that Jesus began this particular teaching by saying, "A man had two sons" (Luke 15:11). Not one, but two.

The younger son occupied the first half of the story with his premature claim on his father's inheritance and lifestyle that would make a weekend in Vegas blush, but the firstborn son was also there. While his backstory was quieter and less clear, we know he was the son who stayed. He was the one who remained with the father, dutifully going into the fields to work and tend his family's land without asking for anything in return (at least, not out loud). By all appearances, he was the good son, and he wore that label with pride and expectation—that is, until his brother came home.

When the youngest returned and was welcomed, fury filled the older son. He paced a path in the dirt outside his family's home and refused to celebrate his brother's homecoming. Inwardly, he cursed and seethed, "I have done everything right, and he's the one who gets the party? That fool? Why did I even try? What was the point?"

To be honest, I get a little angry for him. Why do the right thing if you still end up alone outside the party? Why become the pinnacle of good behavior and excellence when standing on a stage you still feel so dreadfully alone? Like the writer of Ecclesiastes, the imbalance causes us to question, "What do people get for all the toil and anxious striving with which they labor under the sun?" (Ecclesiastes 2:22 NIV). Why be good if "good" is not enough?

These are the questions I asked my freshman year in college when I began to wrestle with anxiety and depression, secretly wondering whether my pain was a punishment after wronging God in some unknown way. This same fury ran through my veins years later as a young mother the day I stood at our back window and watched our pregnant neighbor casually puff at her cigarette on her patio. I seethed knowing it would be her nicotine-covered hands bringing a baby home from the hospital while the unborn son I still carried in my belly would not live past birth, even after I had done everything right. Every time the world grinds against my sense of fairness or hard work ends up hollow, indignance flares within me. Like a toddler, I want to drag my feet and scream into the night sky, "Why try? What is the point?"

Bitterness makes me want to side with the older brother, to reel at the unfairness of it all. But when the fury settles and my mind stops shaking its fist, a gentle Voice inside me whispers, "There is more than one way to be lost."

If we linger in Jesus' story a little longer, what I think we will see is that both sons were prodigals in their own way. Both brothers placed their identities outside the love of the father. One lost himself in greed and sensual indulgence; the other buried himself in duty, diligence, and work. But both men came up lacking. Both men looked for significance, for a belonging crafted by their own hands. One simply had the desperation to make his way back home.

I struggle to identify with the wild living of the younger son, but I see my reflection clearly in the lostness of the elder. I see the way he went into the field day after day, not making waves but silently hoping his good deeds got noticed. I wonder how often he glanced up from tending his crop to see whether his father was watching. Worth and work become so easily tangled and twisted until we struggle to know who we are apart from our doing. But at the end of the day, recognition is a cheap substitute for communion, and acceptance is a temperamental friend.

We can behave our way into many circles, contorting ourselves to fit in, but when "being good" is defined by what is socially acceptable and motivated by desired outcomes rather than the common good, "being good" only gets us through the door. Entrance often comes with a cost, because acceptance asks us to minimize or mask parts of ourselves in order to look like what's expected. Being on the inside can demand that we hide our insecurities, our family histories, our divergent opinions, and our money troubles. We might feel pressure to cover up the shade of our skin, the sound of our voice, the parts of us that seem too big or too small. In the search for acceptance, we often find ourselves hiding right out in the open, and while we might look just like everyone else, we lose ourselves in the process. Like the older brother, we do everything right but still end up alone in the field, kicking up clouds of dirt as anger turns into bitterness that burns beneath the skin.

Divorced from our own identity and distanced from the love of the Father, we end up lost. Every time. The search for acceptance takes us further from our original belonging, because no matter how hard you work, how shiny you become, what awards you collect on your shelves, the high never lasts. The spotlight fades. The trophies collect dust. The labels hide who you really are. As the sun sets and silence rises, you lay your head upon the pillow and sigh, "This too is meaningless, a chasing after the wind" (Ecclesiastes 2:26 NIV).

Who You Are

I do not love meeting new people. But it's not the people. Really. It's those first moments of trying to move from not knowing to kind-of knowing a person that amps up my awkward. Almost every time I am in a situation where I have to introduce myself to someone new, I get sweaty and turn inward, on the verge of a near-existential crisis. *Who. Am. I? Do I stick out my hand and give the laundry list of roles and occupations (wife, mother, writer, daughter, firstborn . . .), or do I respond with a more honest offering? "Hi. I am an introvert and deep feeler who often gets stuck in her head but longs for meaningful connection. Nice to meet you."* People don't seem ready for the fuller answer, but the bullet points seem trite and thin. How are we to find an answer that encompasses all that we are, without overwhelming a stranger all at once? (No, really. Please. Tell me how.)

Identity is tricky, because while unique, we are not formed in isolation. A simple introduction is never simple, because who we are is an amalgamation of our personal wiring, the places we live, the people around us, our histories, and the values we hold. We are human potlucks, each dish and dessert making up the meal of who we are. Parts of our identity are solidified long before that first breath filled our lungs: city of origin, family lineage, the genetic coding imprinted on our DNA, the likelihood that, like my mother and grandmother, I too will have varicose veins. But we are not set-it-and-forget-it creatures. We are both static and active, set and evolving. Formation continues, and like any good Midwestern potluck, who you are becoming can be hard to contain.

But who you are matters to your belonging. The sound of your voice. The shade of your skin. The tiny mole on the tip of your pinky finger. Those details are no accident. While identity is complex, knowing yourself is part of being known. I do not think it was an accident that tacked on to Jesus' teaching to love our neighbors he added two simple words: "as yourself"

(Matthew 22:39). Those two words are not elevated above the admonitions to love God and neighbor, but they also are not absent. They are not forgotten from the equation. Because embedded within the greatest commandment is the reminder of who you are as God's beloved. Love does not ask you to diminish or contort or hide for the sake of acceptance, but to embrace who you are and who you are becoming as a way to better love God and others.

Identity is not an end, but an avenue. It is looking in the mirror to understand the intricacies of a God whose "eyes saw me when I was formless" (Psalm 139:16). It is getting to know and love the Creator and the created through every freckle, every angle, every strand of wild and wiry gray hair. It is becoming acquainted with our own belovedness so that our love for God and each other might swell and grow from what is already in us. It is allowing the full and uncensored view of who you are to become an invitation to move closer, because the more familiar you are with your own reflection, the more you can see your shared humanity in the eyes of another. "For now we see only a reflection as in a mirror, but then face to face. Now I know in part, but then I will know fully, as I am fully known" (1 Corinthians 13:12).

Part and Whole

Several years ago, a few friends and I visited the Magnolia Market silos in Waco, Texas, and as I walked through the doors that day, displayed on one of the walls in large, metal letters was a sign that read:

The World Needs Who You Were Made To Be

At the risk of sounding melodramatic and somewhat cheesy, the truth is that I nearly ugly cried right there on the front steps. The message met me unexpectedly in a moment of intense self-doubt and despair. I stood beneath the sign, mentally repeating the words, as truth I had long buried and forgotten washed over me: to belong to God and to each other, we must also belong to ourselves.

It was not the first time since childhood I had lost sight of who I was (and it will likely not be the last). The lure of acceptance is always singing its sultry song, and we will often be tempted to hum along. But in that moment, I did not realize how lost I felt until those metal letters pointed me back home to the Father, back home to myself, back home to where our common humanity depends on being and giving from the fullness of who we are.

The strange thing about being human is that we must hold our smallness and specialness at the same time. Our flesh comes with both limitations and possibility, inherent goodness and a propensity toward sin, and it is often easier to let one win over the other. It is easier to wrap our identity around half-truths rather than navigate the nuance. But belonging invites us to bring our whole selves into the room.

The apostle Paul described this way of being so well in 1 Corinthians 12, where he talked about the people of God functioning like a body. "Imagine," he said, "that each person is a part (an eye, a hip, a spleen), all coming together to form a greater whole. In the same moment, you are pieces of the body and individual members of it. Distinct and together. Small and essential" (paraphrase; see 1 Corinthians 12:12-27). Your individuality matters because the Spirit is alive in your speci-ficity, and when all those tiny details come together, the sum of our humanity can become a body alight with Love, a manifes-tation of Christ himself. God does not ask us to shrink but to expand, to let our identity become a vessel that we offer in love for "the common good" (1 Corinthians 12:7).

Becoming more ourselves is not self-indulgence, but a way to love. A way to see God. A way to hold our complexities alongside one another. Letting go of external pressures and expectations, the love of the Father invites us to stop searching for acceptance with all its demands, all the ways we lose our-selves in an attempt to be seen, and instead step toward a be-longing that comes to you and says, "You do not have to try so hard. Come home. You were lost but have been found."

3

THE GOD WHO FINDS US

> For what is it
> to be lost
> when every place I graze
> is God's pasture?

DREW JACKSON

For many years, my work in student development required me and my family to live on college campuses. Being able to step out the door of our residence hall apartment into a sea of students, I had a front-row seat to the search for self that so many of us take in our late teens and early twenties. I saw firsthand the internal struggle of young adults as they tried to figure out how to handle their newfound freedoms and make decisions without mom or dad or grandma in the next room. Some students threw themselves into social clubs and activities in an attempt to let anything and everything define them, while others hid in their dorm rooms, distracting themselves with an endless stream of video games (and not enough showers). Leaving home opens up a whole new world, but for many, the lack of familiar faces and places leaves us lost.

Part of my job was responding to campus crises, which usually came under the cloak of night. Regularly, I sat next to young men and women curled into the fetal position on dorm room floors. Gently, I'd ask questions as tears rolled down their cheeks, or we would sit together in silence as they rocked their bodies back and forth. Sometimes, human presence was enough to calm the fears that found them, but other times, the panic and disordered thoughts needed professional care and attention. In those moments before the police or paramedics arrived, I let the ache I felt on their behalf rise like prayers. I spoke words of peace or held hands if they needed it. I sat alongside them as night stretched on, because I too had been there, wondering whether morning would ever cut through the shadows.

Halfway through my own freshman year in college, I began making regular visits to the stone chapel at the center of campus. Like many Midwestern Christian liberal arts institutions, the university was peppered with large brick buildings and sprawling grassy areas where students would play ultimate frisbee or cluster together on a patchwork of blankets. But the chapel was different. Small but stately, a hush lingered there amid the old wooden pews and stained-glass windows. It was a quiet that didn't exist anywhere else on campus, so I went to dampen the noise that had taken over my mind. Ruminating thoughts, fears, and questions played on an endless loop. Anxiety was an unwanted and crippling companion. It pulsed through my chest as I sat in classes and snapped me out of a dead sleep in the middle of the night.

I went to the chapel to pray. I knelt in the din of silence and begged God to take away the pain and the panic. My shoulders slumped beneath the weight of a looming and undefined darkness, as if a blanket had been thrown over my head. A bronze statue of a weeping Jesus, body bent over, was at the front of the chapel. I had never seen a depiction of Jesus so tortured, so wanting, so human. Tears blurred my vision of the Savior before me, but something about his suffering body brought solidarity to my own.

Elbows propped on the wooden prayer bench, I sobbed through salty prayers until I had no tears left to cry. Then, I wiped my face with the back of my hand, squared my shoulders, and returned to my residence hall, hoping this would be the night the darkness would lift. But it didn't. Depression and anxiety followed me like a storm, and shame kept me from asking for help. Not even my roommate knew of the nights I clutched my blankets, wishing for the relief of sleep. Loneliness only amplified the ache, yet I hid the hurt, convinced that shadows fall only on the rebel. I put on a plastic smile, hoping no one would notice the whiteness of my knuckles as I took notes in class or ate sugared cereal in the dining commons, but no amount of shininess saved me from the pain.

The darkness grew darker, until midweek on a blustering January night I called Mom and told her I was coming. I drove the hour and a half through an Indiana snowstorm, only to crumple on the living room floor and weep as my parents knelt next to me. Wordlessly, we sat there. We sat together and cried, and when the tears gave up, so did I. I had been emptied. Mom and Dad walked me up the stairs to my old bedroom, and while the shadows did not lift that evening, as I slipped into my childhood bed and pulled the quilt up around my neck,

I sensed a turning. A fleck of light. A reminder that even at my end I was not alone.

I don't know how you imagined God as a child, whether the Divine was an elusive idea or an image formed by what you'd been told. But for a long time, what kept me from crying out to God in my lostness was fear of the frown I might see across his face. My picture of God was nothing like the bronze statue of Jesus or a loving Creator, but took the form of someone much less approachable, a sort-of ominous combination of Albus Dumbledore and Father Time. I imagined God as a tall man with a long, white beard and a permanent seriousness etched across his face. Quiet. Powerful. A bit elusive and standoffish. Sure, I knew he was good. I wanted to be on his side. Yet I rarely pictured him smiling. Instead, like a guilty kid trying to avoid the gaze of a parent, I did not dare look God directly in the eye.

But the image was wrong. Incomplete, at best. Because who I saw in my greatest moments of desperation looked nothing like a disapproving wizard, but a Savior who lies down next to us in the dirt. Not a God who wants us to clean up our act, but a Father who wants us to be found.

Into the Shadows

What I have come to love most about the parable of the lost sons is the response of the father. Both boys were pretty terrible, one way or another seeking their own gain without thought of their father's loss. The youngest took everything the father had given and squandered it, while the older boy worked his fingers raw to earn his approval, perhaps with a party or a pat on the back. One took the path of every indulgence, while the other constantly strived for the appearance of goodness. But despite this blatant rejection, the father went to find them both. He did not turn away or shake his head or tisk-tisk-tisk his tongue. The father moved closer, inviting both sons to come home.

For a long time, I missed this detail in Jesus' story. I zeroed in on how the forgiving father ran toward the rebel with wide-open arms the moment he appeared on the horizon, but in doing so, I overlooked the quiet way he also went searching for the one who stayed. While the welcome-home party was getting started, the father slipped outside and found his eldest son seething in the shadows. He begged him to come inside. But the son pushed back, "Look, I have been slaving many years for you, and I have never disobeyed your orders, yet you never gave me a goat so that I could celebrate with my friends. But when this son of yours came, who has devoured your assets with prostitutes, you slaughtered the fattened calf for him" (Luke 15:29-30).

I imagine the air between them felt thin, until the father broke the silence by taking yet another step closer. He came near enough so that the young man could see the warmth in his eyes as he whispered, "Son, you are always with me, and everything I have is yours" (Luke 15:31).

Home had always been but a few feet away, the door open and the father waiting. All the son had to do was turn around, and he would have seen that everything he had been working for (worth, recognition, a sense of purpose, love) he already had in the nearness of his father. "Everything I have is yours."

In his book *With*, Skye Jethani writes, "What brought the father joy was not the older son's service but simply his presence—having his son *with* him. This was what the father cared about most, not his property or which son received more. While the sons were fixated on their father's wealth, the father was fixated on his sons." And that's the image of God I want to hold in my mind: a Father who comes to find us.

The Divine invitation has always been rooted in nearness, not rugged will or personal fortitude. Independence is not the pulse of God. He's not the one throwing us into the deep end of the pool, cackling, "Welp, kid . . . ya better learn to swim! And fast!"

God himself bent low, crafting humanity out of the earth and breathing life into our nostrils (Genesis 1:26-27; 2:7). Even when sin and separation threatened to diminish the goodness God set in place, he did not leave us to rot in the misery of our own making. Rather, the Creator remembered the echoes of his goodness he implanted in our bodies and drew near. Over and over again, he has come for us. We read stories of how he found Moses and Abraham, Hagar and David. He set up camp amid the Israelites in the form of cloud and fire, and while God himself was never lost, his presence was with them in their years of wandering and wilderness.

And then there was Jesus. God wrapped flesh around his own divinity and tucked the infant body of his Son inside the delicate folds of a woman's womb. The same earth-tilting power that spoke the world into existence became dependent on humanity itself. He could not get any closer to us than to become one of us. Jesus' humanity and divinity were eternally woven together.

If we lean in and listen closely, all of Jesus' stories about lost things—sons, sheep, coins, you name it—were not to point out how weak and wandering we are or bury us in shame, but for us to know the welcome of the Father. Yes, we are all lost in our own ways, but he is the God who finds us. He is the tender Father who comes to us in the midst of oppressive darkness. He is the Shepherd who carries us on his shoulders. He is the God who comes "near the brokenhearted" and meets us down in the dirt of our lives (Psalm 34:18). He is the God of poetry and painting, song and story, tree and mountaintop. We may be wandering, but he is the God who enters the wilderness to be with us.

I would never wish pain or brokenness on anyone. I would never hope for loss to creep into your life and leave you in shambles. Yet, I have also seen how God approaches these fissures as an opening. For it is often in the darkness that we discover that nearness is in his nature. Our weariness reorients us to his welcome, and our hollow spaces become holy places for Love to dwell.

Down in the Dirt

That desperate night in college, when I drove home to my parents and lay prostrate on the old farmhouse floor, became the first time I allowed others into the raw and bitter wounds that occupied my inner world, but it would not be the last. In many ways, the mental and emotional wrestling I experienced as a new college student was but a prelude to the darkness I would face eight years later. And while I would never invite the things that shatter us, looking back, I am also grateful for the way depression softened me, how it made me aware of the depths of pain so many silently carry in grocery stores and school pickup lines. I am grateful for how my mind began to paint a picture of a truer, kinder God. Grace was not absent, and I often ask myself whether I would have been able to survive the death of our son had it not been for the gentle Father who found me all those years before.

Ben and I found out we were pregnant for our second son on the Fourth of July, and two days before Christmas, our doctors told us his body could not support life outside the womb. Seven weeks later, Carter was born, right in time for a blizzard to blanket Indiana in thick layers of snow and ice. Our town had not seen a storm like that in years, and we made it to the hospital just before the roads became undrivable. Ice pelted the window as our son left my body. Almost immediately, the air inside the room grew warm and sweet. Holiness lingered like a dense fog, as we became witnesses to something heavy but sacred.

The nurse placed all five pounds of our newborn son on my chest, his wrinkly flesh and surprisingly full head of hair just inches from my chin. The weight of him released something in me, a peace that had been buried, tucked into some unknown corner of my soul. Wrapped in the thin hospital blanket, I held Carter a little closer and lifted his face next to mine until his ear pressed against my lips. Only he could hear me whisper, "It's okay. You can be with Jesus." The words came without fore-thought, as if they simply flowed from that unlocked peace as naturally as breathing. I spoke gently to my son, letting him know he did not have to hold on. I repeated the words over and over—for him, but also for me.

For an hour, we watched his chest rise and fall. Each breath was both a blessing and a curse, as we wondered whether the next one would be his last. Friends and family members huddled in the hospital room with us, and we passed Carter around like an old-time church offering basket. I watched as my younger brother took his turn, eyes filling with tears as he placed one large and calloused finger in the delicate palm of our son's tiny hand. The grandmothers fussed as grandmothers do, fidgeting with the blanket to make sure his little feet stayed warm. Mom's mouth creased into one thin, straight line, her lips folded inward as if she were trying to contain a flood behind them. Yet I knew nothing but love was on the other side.

That February morning, a hospital room transformed into holy ground. A Divine presence was so thick, so tangible, that I looked for God among the faces of our family. The sense of his nearness was so real I was sure I could reach out and touch him. What my eyes could not see, my soul knew. God was with us. Even if his body did not materialize, I caught glimpses of his love in the eyes of my mother and brother, in the tears that quietly slipped down the cheeks of our sisters and parents. And it was there in the middle of such palpable love that our son slipped quietly from Ben's arms to the Father's.

For one full but brief moment, we were all Home. Love came near, and my soul recognized its sweetness. I breathed in the scent of what seemed both new and familiar. An ancient longing I had often ignored surfaced and settled, and for the first time, I understood how love could dance between people and God, swirling in and out and through one another interchangeably.

It was an outpouring that tasted like communion, a full-bodied abundance rising amid the bitterness of death.

In the weeks after Carter breathed his last, that hour in the hospital become a life raft as the reality of loss settled in. We never know what the end of ourselves will look like until we get there, and I was a fish whose bones had been yanked out of its body. Our son's absence emptied every space in and around me. It took all my effort to get out of bed and take care of our still-healthy firstborn, a toddler not lacking in energy. I sat on the floor stacking building blocks with an eighteen-month-old Cohen like I had a hundred times before, yet I was constantly aware of the son we had buried beneath the snow-covered earth. Grief hung on my shoulders. My arms burned from wanting, and every time my husband held me close, pain coursed through my swollen chest like a cruel joke, a constant reminder of the baby who should have been at my breast. I longed for the sweet release of sleep, only for grief to return like a tidal wave the moment my eyes fluttered open. Shadows filled my heart and home, and I wanted to disappear into the haze.

I gave very little thought to how I "should" be grieving, not because I was courageous or valiant but rather because the rawness of my emotions left me with very little choice. Everything I had spent years trying to hide was on full display. But it was there, in that tender state, that God found me yet again. Instead of disapproval, I saw the sparkle of love in his eyes. I sensed the warmth of his nearness. His arms were not crossed against his chest, but open and inviting. He did not come to me with furrowed brow and wagging finger but with a gentle smile and hand resting on my shoulder. Even now, I can see the tears of love welling up in his eyes.

Past Sarah had put forth great effort to be shiny and acceptable, but in the throes of grief, I learned how to be loved in the dark. Sitting in the remains of all I had so carefully planned and what I thought I deserved, God met me in the hollows, and instead of leaving me there, he simply sat down beside me. He held me in the muck and the mire. While the grief did not disappear, my soul knew the words of the psalmist, "Even the darkness is not dark to you. The night shines like the day; darkness and light are alike to you" (Psalm 139:12).

The God Who Sees

Tattoos have become a way for me to let myself be marked, an act not of rebellion but of surrender. I am a wandering creature, prone to worry and fear and doubt, and like the Israelites in the desert, I need visible reminders of who I am and where I belong. I need pillars of cloud by day and fire by night. I need to remember that God is with me—even here, even now, no matter what.

Several years after we lost our son, I tattooed "El Roi" on my forearm. This name of God comes from Genesis 16 when Hagar, an Egyptian slave girl, finds herself alone in the desert, pregnant, hurting, and out of options. There beside an unlikely desert stream, God met her. When no one else was searching, God came close, not only hearing her "cry of affliction" but also reminding her of her worth (Genesis 16:11). He handed her hope, revealing that the child she carried—though forced upon her—was not a blemish but a blessing that would transform a family and a nation.

And even though God asked Hagar to go back to where she had come from (a request even now I struggle to understand), that day she named God "El Roi," which means the "God who sees me," because there in the desert with knees too weak to stand, Hagar marveled, "In this place, have I actually seen the one who sees me?" (Genesis 16:13).

Being seen by God changes everything, because our belonging is rooted in a God who sees. In his gaze, we can know our lives have a witness.

I had "El Roi" etched into my arm because, like Hagar, I need to remember I am not alone. I need regular reminders that my belonging is anchored in a God who not only crafted me out of the dirt but also sat down in it with me. Our lostness is no match for his presence. Because even in our darkest nights or deepest shadows, when we feel we belong to nothing and no one, we are never outside God's nearness. There is no darkness so dark that God will not enter it. There is no emptiness so full of void that God cannot dwell within it. The Father has always been with us, and everything he has is ours.

4

EVERYTHING IS YOURS

> The boundary lines have fallen for me
> in pleasant places;
> surely I have a delightful inheritance.

PSALM 16:6 NIV

Many days I wake up early to write or to read. Usually, I can sneak in an hour or two before requests for breakfast or backpacks begin. But recently, our seven-year-old son snuck into the office and peeked over my shoulder as I worked at the computer. The sky was black outside the window. His little voice broke the quiet tapping of the keys, "Mom, what is belonging?"

I swiveled the desk chair toward him and pulled him onto my lap. His blue eyes searched my face, and I smiled. Here I was writing a book about belonging but struggling to find the right words to answer his simple question. Finally, I told him, "Belonging is when we are safe, seen, and loved, where we can be ourselves."

He rested his head on my shoulder, "Oh, you mean, like home?"

"Yes, exactly," I held him closer. "Belonging is just like home."

When I close my eyes and imagine coming home to God, I squint to see what is written on the mat outside his front door. What greeting would we find as we step over the threshold? I recently saw an online shop selling "Christian welcome mats" that offered a number of options: "Bless This House," "Jesus Loves You," or "Before You Break Into My House, Stand Outside & Get Right with Jesus. Tell Him You're On Your Way" (complete with handgun). You cannot make this stuff up.

But the more I get to know the abundant and persistent love of God, I believe what we'd find on God's front porch (perhaps next to clay pots filled with red geraniums) are three words: You are welcome.

Whether you come as the prodigal or as the performing older brother, you are welcome.

Whether your feet are bare or wearing Valentino, you are welcome.

Whether you sing in the choir or in the shower, you are welcome.

Whether you take pills or make pills or avoid all forms of medicine, you are welcome.

Young or old, black or white, near or far, healthy or sick, you are welcome.

Whatever brought you to the door, you are welcome.

All of you.

The mat doesn't say "Wipe Your Feet" or "Leave Your Problems on the Porch." There are no disclaimers for what you must do or how you must behave before entry. (There are certainly no threatening weapons.) The message of Jesus has always been rooted in welcome. "Knock, and the door will be opened to you" (Matthew 7:7) did not begin as a kitschy saying but as a sincere invitation to come home, because Jesus knew that the Father would not pause to fling that narrow door wide open and greet whoever stood there with a smile, "Come on in. Everything I have is yours" (Luke 15:31, my phrasing).

I don't know about you, but these words feel like inhaling freedom. I close my eyes as the exhale eases my muscles and my mind. It is as if the sweet love of God cups my face in his hands and says, "Child, you do not have to try so hard." His eyes are warm and sincere. I believe him, so I step over the mat and make my way inside.

The welcome of God changes everything.

As our feet cross the threshold, we settle into the love of the Father and discover how to relate not only to him but also to ourselves. We see who we are more clearly—our wants and our weaknesses, what we have to offer the world and the ways we are prone to wandering. We become familiar with how we are wired, as human people with "eternity in their hearts" (Ecclesiastes 3:11). We find a belonging that does not hinge upon place or people, but is a love we carry with us, just as we are and who we are becoming. This is where we belong.

A Disclaimer

Before we get much further, I want to make sure I do not inadvertently paint life with God as a life of ease. That image is one of the many false concepts I have had to undo in adulthood, as outcomes did not match my expectations. While I do not want to diminish the extravagance of God's invitation or the fullness we find on the other side (peace is one of the many mysteries of the Divine), a life with God is not without problems. Nearness to God does not mean we will never be lonely for human connection or that self-doubt will not plague us around every corner. It does not mean that accidents will not happen, death will not rob us, or that we will suddenly become less awkward at social gatherings. (At least, that has not happened for me yet.)

Choosing to make our home in God, while good, does not mean life will turn out just the way we want. This kind of gumball machine theology goes against the very life and words of Jesus, who on his way to death reminded his disciples (and us), "You will have suffering in this world" (John 16:33). What you put in is no guarantee of what will pop out the other end, so when we make our pursuit of God about anything other than God himself, we find ourselves disillusioned and disappointed, because life with God is not a pill to consume, but an invitation to commune.

But here's the bright spot: stepping into the Father's welcome offers us a haven. We are safe. We belong in him no matter the storm that rages outside or within us, because like the psalmists (who were well acquainted with grief and loneliness and regrets of all kind), we can declare as the wind and rain pelt us in the face, "Keep me safe, my God, for in you I take refuge" (Psalm 16:1 NIV). When night closes in around us, we can "wait for the LORD," certain that the sun will rise again and we will "see the LORD's goodness in the land of the living" (Psalm 27:13-14).

Because like a mother bird, God covers us with an outstretched wing, and sooner or later beneath those wild and mysterious feathers, we find abundance in nothingness, peace amid pushback, stillness as life swirls around us, and compassion cropping up in the dirt of disappointment. The Father welcomes us to sit down with him in the gray spaces of our lives, knowing that we are both broken and beloved and these realities point us to a good and abundant God of refuge. We belong no matter what.

Weak and Worthy

Our youngest son was born with ambiguous eyes. In some lights, you would swear they are green or brown, but upon closer inspection, each little orb appears to be a swirl of many colors, a tiny earth inside his eyes. Most days, we declare them "hazel," but really, his eyes contain multitudes, complexities that are not easily named on a short list of color options on a doctor's form. We check the box, but inwardly we know there is more to the story.

Modern culture does not do a great job at leaving room for complexity. But like our son's eyes, humanity is far from being easily contained and categorized. Each of us is a swirl of often-competing realities, and our inability to let these realities coexist often keeps us from belonging to God, to ourselves, and to each other. We have become more concerned with labels than love.

Over the last twenty years, I have often found myself conflicted as two pervasive and contradictory messages have plagued not only our relationships but also our interior lives:

You are enough.

You are not enough.

Take one trip to the local bookstore's self-help or Christian living section, and you can find plenty of gurus who preach either a gospel of self-love or self-abatement. A simple skim of the titles would leave any person confused: Am I too much or too little? Too amazing or too worthless? Too good or too sinful? Too empowered or too needy? (Please tell me what I am!)

Identity gets lost in competing messages that push us to one corner or the other. Our sense of self gets ripped apart because we believe we must check a box, and as a result, our belonging suffers. We do not step into the fullness of the Father because we believe we are too much of one thing: too virtuous or too fallen. Too needy or too proud. Too full of our own goodness or too far from it. Too proud or too full of shame. We try to cram our humanity into either-or containers, hoping to find safety and acceptance, but the only thing these "too much" statements do is teach us to see ourselves and others as either good or bad, the hero or the villain, the prodigal or the eldest son, enough or not enough. In those tidy boxes, we lose the complexity of who we are and fail to make room for who we are yet to be.

In the year following our son Carter's death, I was like a pinball that couldn't settle into a clear sense of self. I drew the curtains and hid beneath the covers, unable to will myself out of bed. The retching pain of grief made me well acquainted with my finitude, all the days my brain and body wanted to down the orange bottle of pain pills and disappear, at least for a little while. Yet God met me. Like a mother rubbing the back of a crying child, God's presence soothed me, "Be still." His love washed over me with abundance, the hairs on my arms rising in remembrance that I am a child whose fibers were formed in the image of a Creator God. With God, I was not weak or worthy. I was both. In him, I could look at myself in the mirror and see those deep, dark circles around my eyes not with shame but with compassion. Yes, I was broken, but I was also beloved.

Coming home to God allows you to erase the lines you so often draw around yourself and brings you "out to a spacious place" where in the same sentence you can be too much and too little, enough and yet not enough (Psalm 18:19). When the Father whispers "everything is yours," you can let the breath of God fill your lungs because you do not have to perform your way into his presence but can come just as you are. You can know that before light touched your skin for the very first time, God saw your unformed body within the folds of your mother and declared, "You are good." You do not have to choose whether you are weak or worthy, an image of God or a person in process, because you are both. You are woven from the welcome of God, a person in whom Love chooses to dwell. There is no checkbox for such extravagant grace. There is only freedom.

A Delightful Inheritance

God receives and celebrates every broken and beloved soul who knocks, but he does not leave us there on the front porch. "Everything I have is yours" is not a front-porch kind of life. Abundance is part of God's nature, and the Father is continually waving us to come "farther up and further in." The welcome does not end at the door, because within the Father's love, we are not only found but formed.

God's belonging works its way into our beings. Under his merciful wing, we become bearers of his likeness. We are no longer visitors but heirs to "a delightful inheritance" as he moves us further into his love (Psalm 16:6 NIV). Truly, my brain cannot contain the both/and nature of this spiritual reality, that at the same time we are both accepted as we are and being molded more and more into the likeness of the Father. Like lost socks, God's love picks us up and turns us right side out, so that the fundamental elements of who we are remain intact, but who we are becoming reflects the deepest truths of who we were made to be.

You belong. (Full stop. Period. End of sentence.) And also: you are still becoming. You are an actual human person who is stretching, flexing, and finding your feet in the world. But you are not alone. Spiritual formation is our inheritance, not only a taste of a rich and vibrant belonging but also an invitation to become like the Father. As Henri Nouwen writes,

> Becoming like the heavenly Father is not just one important aspect of Jesus' teaching, it is the very heart of his message. . . . As long as we belong to this world, we will remain subject to its competitive ways and expect to be rewarded for all the good we do. But when we belong to God, who loves us without conditions, we can live as he does. The great conversion called for by Jesus is to move from belonging to the world to belonging to God.

As God replicates his welcome in and through us, we settle into the fullness of our skin, while at the same time, we become shaped more and more into Christ's likeness, albeit in slow and often grinding ways. We plant our feet firmly in who we are but are given new eyes with which to see, living no longer as people of scarcity but as people of abundance because this is our hope and our inheritance. Love, joy, peace, patience, kindness, goodness, gentleness, faithfulness, self-control—everything is ours. As we breathe the very breath of God, he becomes our boundary line, and as his vastness transforms our void, we let go of urgency, embrace mystery, and open our palms wide with generosity. We are both weak and worthy here in the middle because we belong as daughters and sons, but we are becoming like Christ, day by day, little by little, as God patiently inches us closer to himself and to one another, thus narrowing the gap between the earthly and the eternal.

The welcome is for us and within us and then turns us outward. As we are held, we learn to hold as Divine love settles further into our souls and then frees us to be the person we want others to be for us. We belong, and that belonging works its way into who we are and how we relate to the wider world.

5

A MOBILE HOME

> **What a long time it can take
> to become the person one has always been!**

PARKER PALMER

For most of my childhood, my grandma and step-grandpa lived in a single-wide trailer, just a few miles up the county road from our house in Auburn, Indiana. I loved visiting Grandma Dottie. Without fail, Grandma would greet me at the door and pull me so close my face became buried in her ample chest, and then, with a sparkle of mischief in her eye, she would nudge me gently past her latest pet parakeet toward the snack cabinet filled with Little Debbie snacks. (Grandma always had oatmeal cream pies.) I'd plop down on the couch with a book, the grandfather clock ticking just over my shoulder, while Grandma sat in her recliner to watch her stories—always *The Young and the Restless* and never *Days of Our Lives*. That's how it was at Grandma's house, and the moment I walked through the door, I was home.

Yet the reality is that Grandma's house was not a house at all. While it rested on concrete footers, nothing about the trailer was attached to the ground. I am pretty sure that if I were to have peeled back the vinyl skirting that wrapped around the bottom, I would have seen wheels or a steel structure that could have easily been transported. But that didn't matter. Looking back, Grandma's house could have been anywhere—downtown by the railroad tracks, in the middle of a corn field, nestled right in our backyard. The setting didn't change what was inside, because I knew that no matter where Grandma's house was parked, she would still be there, with her squeaky screen door, pet birds, and oatmeal cream pies. Just the way I liked it.

All these years later, I am beginning to realize that belonging is very much like Grandma's house. It is not dependent on a particular person, place, or idea. It is not a status to possess or attain like a merit badge. Situations change. People change. And we can let them. Because despite the uncertainty that comes with being human together, belonging is a welcome we carry with us.

A Place of Welcome

When I think again about Jesus' story of the lost sons, I notice a couple things. First, the invitation of the father was not dependent on his children coming back to him. He did not wait for them to cross his threshold before he welcomed them to come inside. Rather, the father stepped off his front porch to go in pursuit of both his boys; he carried the warmth of welcome with him. He wanted to walk with them back home through the door.

Here, in the actions of the father, we discover that belonging is mobile. Movement is baked into the word. Back in the mid-fourteenth century, the word *belong* was originally composed of two main parts: *bi-*, a prefix indicating thoroughness, and *long* (or *longen*), which is translated "to go." Put together, *belong* is a verb that means "to go along with" or "properly relate to." In other words, belonging is both being and doing, both who you are and what you carry with you. It is part essence and part movement. It is the father saying "everything I have is yours" but still taking steps toward his sons (Luke 15:31).

The second thing I see when I look at this story through the lens of belonging is less of a certainty and more of a question. Two questions, really: *Who am I in this parable? And who am I becoming?* The first question leads me to understand myself better, to identify with one son or the other so that I can let myself be found. Here I find the "be" part of belonging. But the second question I am slower to answer, because it begs me to consider not only who I am but also who I am moving toward. Which person am I becoming? Which person does my soul long to emulate?

When I step back from the story, I do not want to be the sons at all. Rather, I am drawn to the father. The more I see the look of love in his eyes, the more I am compelled to carry his welcome. Henri Nouwen articulated this shift toward the father so well. He writes: "Why pay so much attention to the sons when it is the father who is in the center and when it is the father with whom I am to identify? Why talk so much about being like the sons when the real question is: Are you interested in being like the father?"

From the delicate corners of the soul, the heart answers yes. Because while we might see our brokenness in the sons, we see our hope and wholeness in the father. Instead of being filled with shame or the pressure to perform, we begin to sense the inherent invitation that comes with becoming more and more like God himself. We can feel the welcome bubbling up within us, as "we all, with unveiled faces, are looking as in a mirror at the glory of the Lord and are being transformed into the same image from glory to glory" (2 Corinthians 3:18).

The welcome of God is for you, but it is also within you. The invitation begins as sons and daughters, as we let ourselves be found and come to eat from the abundance God has to offer. But belonging does not leave us there, content to become bloated when the feast is meant to be shared. As we become more like our own Father, belonging moves us toward each other. It guides us toward a posture that lets the love of God not only dwell within us but also form us more and more into a place of welcome as we move throughout the world. To belong is to become an extension of his Divine embrace. You are the welcome.

The more you see that welcome in who you are and who you are becoming, the more you invite a kingdom "on earth as it is in heaven" into the middle of your ordinary, everyday life (Matthew 6:10). You discover the fullness of what it means to "love the Lord your God with all your heart, with all your soul, and with all your mind" within the small moments of loving "your neighbor as yourself" around loud and rowdy kitchen tables, in grocery store lines, or while raking the leaves beyond your own backyard. You begin to see evidence of the Spirit as "love, joy, peace, patience, kindness, goodness, faithfulness, gentleness, and self-control" rise to the surface of your reactions (Galatians 5:22-23). You find the unlikely joy that comes with being the kind of person we want others to be for us, not for the accolades or the outcomes, but simply because we are following the uncommon but wonderful ways of Jesus, who showed us that it truly is "more blessed to give than to receive" (Acts 20:35).

It does not mean we do not want to be wanted. It does not mean we do not also carry the desire to be safe, seen, respected, and enjoyed. That is part of being human. But instead of caving in on ourselves in those moments of loneliness or isolation, we learn to view them through the lens of welcome, seeing the sacredness not only in our need for each other but also as an invitation to walk each other Home.

Not a Welcome Mat

I want to pause here for a moment to clarify what welcome is not. Simply put, you are a person of welcome, not a welcome mat. You are not a place for people to wipe their shoes or tread on. You do not have to prostrate yourself—to make yourself less—in order to take a posture of warmth, generosity, and openness.

Becoming the love of the Father does not mean that you have to be all things to all people. We can remember that Jesus himself had boundaries. He had his closest friends as well as his time away from the crowds. Jesus modeled what it looked like to say healthy yeses and healthy noes, and within God's welcome, we can have freedom to do the same.

Similarly, welcome is a posture, not a performance. Your worth is inherent because of who you are as God's beloved. When tempted to let welcome become your work, remember the words of the father to his son, "You are always with me, and everything I have is yours" (Luke 15:31). You do not get any bonus points for being more compassionate to more people. No one is keeping a tally of your self-sacrifice. Instead, you can let yourself be found and formed by embracing the welcome of God within you and letting it change the way you relate to the people already in your midst. Belonging is not your work, but a way of being in the world.

Last of all, know that you do not have to park your home on land where you are not received. You have the freedom to "shake the dust off your feet" in places where you are not safe or wanted. Yes, following Jesus often comes with struggles, disappointments, and rejections, but you do not have to stay and make yourself a martyr or let yourself be dragged through the dirt. You can go, and under the umbrella of Jesus' blessing, "Let your peace return to you" (Matthew 10:13).

A Way Forward

So now what? How do we move forward? How do we reorient ourselves away from the myth that belonging is a place or person to attain and toward a way of welcome?

Nearly every time I have made a life change, the decision came on the heels of desperation. Three out of our four sons were potty trained because I had just one too many days of changing diapers and declared in a moment of need, "Done! We're done with diapers. You wear underwear now." The system was not perfect. I invested in a steam mop. But there was something about getting to the end of myself that allowed me to make a needed shift. That moment of clarity—the deep awareness that old ideas and practices were no longer working—became the impetus I needed to look for a different way. The need became a catalyst.

Perhaps that is where you are now. Perhaps you are tired of surface relationships or sense loneliness rising up within you, that old burning in your chest as you imagine what it might be like to be settled in your skin, to know the Spirit of God within you as you discover how to hold and be held. You are thinking, *Okay, this is all great. But how?*

I can almost hear the questions coming through the page, because they are as familiar as my own. The idea that you are a place of welcome is a concept we can think nice thoughts about all day long, but how do we move it from our heads into our feet and fingertips? How can we disentangle ourselves from ways of thinking that fail to move us closer to God or to each other? What spiritual practices can we embrace?

Over the last few years, I have asked these very same questions, wondering, *What does welcome look like?* as I make my way into a room. I have read (and reread) the stories of Jesus, taking note of his presence among people. I have revisited old conversations with college students, young moms, and pastors, looking for threads to pull. I have geeked out on research studies and books about research studies. At home and at church and at coffee shops, I have paid attention to the people and places that make me feel safe, seen, respected, and enjoyed, not because they alone were the answer, but because, like a bloodhound, I have been intent on sniffing out the essence of Home.

The hard news first: belonging is not linear and cannot be prescribed. There is no four-step plan or magic pill. Peopling is complex and winding, and we must leave room for nuance. Like waves against the sand, slowly and gently forming us, belonging is forever shifting along the shore. Life changes. Our capacity changes. Relationships take an unexpected turn. If we do not allow our belonging to bend and flex and shape us into who we are becoming, we can lose sight of the welcome within us.

But the good news for all of us wanting a way forward is that belonging is not void of action. While "being" is part of the equation (and quite frankly, the part I like best), let's not forget that the word *belong* is a verb that implies movement. It is not static. It does not sit and wait, hoping others will come through the door. There are things we can do to cultivate a life of welcome.

In the space we still have together (beginning in part two), I want to give us something to hold on to as we plot a path forward and reimagine how we relate, and we'll do that by looking at both postures and practices of belonging. They are not hard-and-fast rules, but invitations. The posture chapters (which begin with "From") take a closer look at how certain mindsets might be injuring our connectedness and offer an alternative approach. The postures invite us to look inward at the *be* part of belonging. We will consider our inner attitudes and reflect on how those perspectives impact our relationships. Each posture is followed by a corresponding practice. Here we look at the ways we can intentionally move (or *longen*) toward God and each other in the midst of our everyday lives, because like muscles slowly formed over time, these intentional movements meet us where we are and shape who we are becoming.

I encourage you to go slowly and tenderly with yourself and others. Know that each posture and practice leaves plenty of room for grace, and what works for me may not work perfectly for you. Only you can know the rumblings of your own soul. All I can do is invite you to keep your ear to the ground. Pay attention to the nudges, and remember that like the changing tides, belonging is both a pressing in and a pulling back. We never really arrive, but we can let ourselves be moved.

Part II

HOW WE RELATE

Alone, all alone
Nobody, but nobody
Can make it out here alone.

MAYA ANGELOU

Dear friends, if God loved us in this way,
we also must love one another.

1 JOHN 4:11

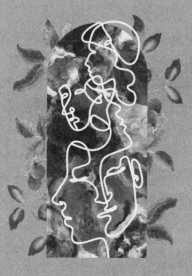

6

FROM LACK TO LONGING

Longing itself is a creative and spiritual state.

SUSAN CAIN

It was 5:30 a.m. on a Sunday morning. I stood on a street corner in the residential part of downtown Greenville, South Carolina, suitcase nestled close to my legs. "Two more minutes," I half-yawned, half-whispered to my friend Kristina, who stood next to me as we waited for our ride.

I was glad Kristina was there. After gathering with a few other writing friends for a weekend of good food and good conversation, we were headed to the airport to catch our respective flights home. Like that moment after a holiday meal when you finally sit down on the couch and undo your pants a little, my soul felt more than full. Our weekend had satiated a hunger I did not know how to verbalize as I stood there in the darkness. The level of connection and meaningful discussion far surpassed my expectations, an abundance that held breathless wonder of the sacred.

Car lights approached as a white sedan appeared out of the darkness and slowed to a stop next to the curb. Within minutes, our driver gathered the suitcases in the trunk as Kristina and I settled into the back seat, and we set off for the airport. Relative silence filled the space between us. While I was content to let it linger, the quiet did not last long. Our driver—a young man presumably in his late twenties—seemed eager to make conversation. I sighed the deep sigh of the tired and travel worn. It was dark. I had not had a drop of coffee, and to top off my dread, I do not like making small talk at noon on a Tuesday, let alone 5:30 a.m. on a Sunday. But this stranger did not deserve my saltiness, so I obliged.

As conversation unfolded, the dark-haired man told us he had come to the city as a traveling physical therapist. When he spoke about his PT work and his patients' progress, his voice grew warm and tender. I could see only the back of his head, and yet I knew he was smiling. Compassion emanated all around him.

My head tilted to the side, my left eyebrow lifting as curiosity bubbled up within me. This man appeared smart. Kind. Capable. He was assumably well compensated for his day job, because he spoke about driving for Uber as if it were something he did on the side, not as a necessity. Yet, there we were in his white, well-maintained sedan before dawn on a Sunday.

"So why do you drive for Uber?" I asked. (Yes, perhaps that was a little too intimate a question to ask a stranger at 5:30 a.m., but I warned you I do not do small talk well. Forgive me.)

Eyes still fixed on the highway in front of us and seemingly unfazed by my probing, the young man replied, "I move a lot, so it's hard to get to know people, and I'm too old for the clubs and stuff. I drive so I can talk to people." And then he added, "You guys are the nicest I've picked up in two weeks."

My heart sank. I had climbed into his car feasting off a weekend of deep connection with friends, only to encounter a man so hungry for the presence of others that he willingly woke up before dawn for a chance to talk with strangers.

His words struck something deep in me. The more I examined my reaction, the way it pressed heavy on my chest, the more I realized the feelings that initially masqueraded as pity or compassion weren't really those things at all. The ache was too familiar. Too close. Transcendent, even. No, the groans that surfaced were those of my own wanting. His desire for connection echoed my own, as if an ancient drum reverberated through the both of us. A rhythm primal yet eternal.

His longing for belonging was my own. I knew it well.

A few minutes later, we pulled up to the airport. Our driver jumped out of the vehicle to grab our suitcases and as he slid the roller bag my way, I thanked him. Then he was gone. The young man drove off to pick up another rider before we had even seen the sun.

As I watched him leave, the subtle burning in my chest remained. His honesty had pulled back the layers of my own wanting, forcing me to look at the ache rather than bury it beneath the self-doubt that so often rides on my shoulders. Standing there in the harsh glow of the airport lighting, my desire for belonging was laid bare, but instead of a picture of lack, what I saw was a beautiful longing.

Design, Not Deficiency

Looking back, I recognize that a subtle shift began in my thinking that day. While rationally I knew I was not alone in my want of human connection, what I did not realize is that I had been treating my longing like an enemy. I had perceived my want of place and people as a hole in need of patching, a symptom of a disease I did not want others to know I had. I thought longing was nothing more than an indication of lack, and I had trained myself to look away. Who wants to be reminded of all the things that they are not?

But lack and longing are not the same.

I like to think of lack and longing as two pairs of glasses. The differences are often subtle on the surface. Both reveal our felt loneliness, wounds, questions, and discontent. Both can be painfully vulnerable and uncomfortable and leave us wishing for those days of blissful blurriness, before we knew the depths of our desire for a place and a people. However, the prescriptions in these two pairs of glasses are not the same.

The lens of lack is thick with scarcity—the belief in never enough. Scarcity loves to suffocate, cloaking our relationships and decisions in fear and distorting the image of God in and around us. It takes and takes and takes until all we can see is what we do not have. But the Divine deals not in scarcity but in abundance. Despite all the ways lack leaves us fearful and grasping for shriveled-up versions of connectedness, the lens of longing helps us see past the hollowness and hear the Father as he whispers, "Everything I have is yours" (Luke 15:31).

Lack shrinks, but longing expands.

Lack isolates, but longing tilts our heads up and out.

Lack side-eyes the competition and leans toward striving, but longing holds out its hands.

In all the ways lack paints a portrait of less-than, longing reminds us we are God's masterpiece.

Lack hides in the shadows, but longing lets the light in.

Both lack and longing can sting. An ache is still an ache, and due to all our human differences, the want within us can arrive in myriad ways. Mine often comes in a wave of emotion (usually envy) or self-doubt, while yours might arrive like an eighth-grade math teacher, wagging a finger and demanding that you "show your work!" Only you can perceive the gaps within yourself, the moments when your soul echoes with wanting.

But when the ache arrives, the lens through which we see our desire to belong influences not only what we do with it but also how we relate. The way we see that twinge of loneliness changes the way we enter a room. Because while the lens of lack is shadowed, causing us to cave inward, longing invites us to look up and out.

When I was a child, a piece of stained-glass art hung in one of our farmhouse windows. I loved to sit on the steps next to the glass and stare out at the backyard, because no matter the weather outside the window, the glass painted the world in bright blues and saturated oranges. Always beautiful. Always warm and full of promise.

Longing is like looking through stained glass. The image is still there. The situation has not changed. We still want to be safe, seen, respected, and enjoyed. But instead of an ache that is beige and bleak, we see a prismatic invitation into more. Longing changes the narrative, showing us that the desire to belong is not a deficiency, but part of a God-given design.

Where Longing Leads Us

In grad school, we studied Abraham Maslow's hierarchy of needs, which teaches that being in a posture of need is part of being a person. We all need food in our bellies. We all crave looks of love. We all require sleep. Fragility is woven into the fibers of who we are. But often, pitted against Westernized ideals that elevate strength, greatness, and independence, people who express their needs are often met with looks of pity rather than compassion or empathy. They are given the ol' "bless her heart" rather than a "yes, me too." I have been just as guilty of looking down on those who are struggling, wishing they would just pull it together.

But when need is not seen within the context of our shared humanity, we buy into the idea that our weakness is not welcomed. We square our shoulders, take a deep breath, and puff out our chests in an attempt to appear stronger than we are. We learn to hide the very things that make us human.

Scripture seems to agree with Maslow (at least, with the idea that being a person with needs is universal). Page after page of the Bible is peppered with stories and songs and prophesies filled with ache. We see echoes of our own longing in the cries of Hannah as she wept for a son, in the uncensored confessions of Job, and in Jesus himself as he asked the Father to "take this cup." One peek into the Psalms brings us face to face with all-too-familiar wanting:

My God, my God, why have you abandoned me?
Why are you so far from my deliverance
and from my words of groaning? (Psalm 22:1)

Lord, my every desire is in front of you;
my sighing is not hidden from you. (Psalm 38:9)

As a deer longs for flowing streams,
so I long for you, God.
I thirst for God, the living God. (Psalm 42:1-2)

God, you are my God; I eagerly seek you.
I thirst for you;
my body faints for you
in a land that is dry, desolate, and without water.
(Psalm 63:1)

The human yearning contained within God's Word reveals that, even across cultures and time, longing speaks an eternal language our souls can understand, and while lack leads us to dead ends, longing guides us Home. As psychiatrist Curt Thompson writes, "Desire is the very substance of our created being to which God is calling. He is calling out our desire in order to redeem it and to make it the leading edge of the renewal of all things."

Nowhere is this invitation more apparent than in the first few lines of Jesus' Sermon on the Mount. Sitting with his newly formed group of disciples, a cluster of ragtag fishermen, a despised tax collector, and other everyday men who might have been wondering why they had been asked to come along at all, Jesus painted a picture of his kingdom—a people who do not posture themselves in greatness but who participate in the kingdom on their knees:

Blessed are the poor in spirit,
for the kingdom of heaven is theirs.

Blessed are those who mourn,
    for they will be comforted.
Blessed are the humble,
    for they will inherit the earth.
Blessed are those who hunger and thirst for righteousness,
    for they will be filled. (Matthew 5:3-6)

Jesus seemed to be telling them (and us) that need—the posture the world deems as weakness—is the very path that leads us Home. Longing is not lack but a groaning toward God's abundance, leading us toward the eternity embedded in our hearts.

The same is true of the need to belong. Your entire being cries out for communion (the very essence of our original design) because you were crafted to be known in deep and abiding ways. Your need is not a nuisance, but the very thing that is pointing you toward the love for which you were created.

By trading a lens of lack for a lens of longing, you peel back the layers often covered by scabs of scarcity to discover the abundance of God. A vastness without void. A feast with no end. You discover that desire is not a deficiency but your humanity leaning toward what is holy. Longing in and of itself is a welcoming, and the holy end of wanting is with-ness. While eternal longing often leaves us with an ache here on earth, our fragility becomes the place where we are found.

Looking Inward

Now that we have entered the "yes, but how" part of the book, I want to offer some potential next steps to embrace and extend belonging. At the end of each chapter, you will find an invitation to reflect or a practice to try out. Feel free to pick these up if they resonate or let them go if they feel like another to-do on an over-full list.

Moving from lack to longing often requires us to get gut-level honest with ourselves, because on the surface, the two can look very much the same. Perhaps a good first step is to ask yourself: *What is my relationship with my desires? When the ache of loneliness or isolation surfaces, how do I respond?* You may want to journal your thoughts or talk it through with a trusted friend, but give yourself some space to sit with your responses and consider whether you're more inclined toward a lens of lack or of longing.

7

THE ART OF NAMING

To name is to love. To be Named is to be loved.

MADELEINE L'ENGLE

Early in our marriage, Ben and I moved to the northeast side of Indianapolis, where we bought our first home. It had been a foreclosure, and the previous owners appeared to have moved out rather reluctantly, leaving some less-than-lovely remnants of their anger behind. I will spare you the details. Let's just say the house needed work, so we poured ourselves into remodeling. Most evenings and weekends were spent painting walls, ripping up flooring, and reimagining what the home could be. Busy with the work, I did not think much about the fact we had moved to not only a new neighborhood but also a large city where we knew next to no one. That is, until one Friday night when I found myself alone in a new house.

Ben was out of town, and as I sat on the couch that evening, phone in hand, I realized I had no one to call. Not a friend. Not an acquaintance. Not a neighbor. Not a family member within a two-hour radius. Loneliness washed over me like molasses, weighing hard and heavy upon my shoulders. I don't know how long I sat there, contemplating what to do next. But in that moment, the ache began to swirl.

On any given day, in new places and spaces, my personality is hardwired to see all the ways I do not fit. Heart pumping, hands clenched, my mind rehearsing conversations that have not yet happened, I try to appear calm and cool. ("For goodness' sake, Sarah. Be. Cool.") But eyes glued to the floor, my mind twists and turns and inevitably caves inward before I have even given the room a chance. Whether my outsider status is real or imagined, lack paints the room in dark hues of shame and envy, and the resulting internal narrative goes a little something like this:

You are the odd person out.

You are the outlier, the wallflower, the one-off who can't figure out how to work the room.

You are too much and not enough.

You will never fit in.

When I am lonely or relationships do not come easily, I assume the problem is in me. Or worse, the problem *is* me. And much like that night home alone in Indianapolis, I end up paralyzed as lack begins to circle.

But we are not at lack's mercy. There is always a deeper longing waiting underneath to lead us closer to God and to each other. But first, the longing needs a name.

What's in a Name?

I am a natural-born feeler, so when the desire to belong rises within me, my body and emotions register its presence long before my brain has had a chance to recognize what is happening. For most of us, longing rarely comes with a name badge. It does not stick out its hand and introduce itself, "Oh, hey there. My name is Safety, middle name Acceptance. Good to meet you." No, the longing for connection often arrives as an undercurrent. A little twinge. A growing ache inside the chest. A small thought pressing up against your forehead as you wonder, *What does he have that I don't?*

As a result, most days we can easily bypass the longing. We can shirk away from the ache or distract ourselves with things like house projects, online shopping, or spreadsheets. But when we ignore the ache and do not wrap words around our desires, we detach ourselves from the goodness of our longings.

Shakespeare might have contested that the practice of naming things is irrelevant, that no matter what you name a rose or a sunset or your new Labrador puppy, its sweetness remains intact. But I tend to (respectfully) disagree with Shakespeare. Naming is one of the most important things we do as humans. Naming is how we make sense of the world—both the seen and the unseen. It is how we assign value and find common language. By wrapping words around our longings, we begin not only to receive them and let them tell us something eternal but also to imagine how we might offer these desires as a gift to the wider world.

In the story of creation, one of the first tasks God gave humankind was to name the creatures. One by one, winged animals with knobby knees and burly beasts were brought to Adam to "see what he would call it" (Genesis 2:19). I imagine the sparkle in God's eyes as he watched and waited to hear the names the man would give to each wild being. God could have said, "Hey, Adam, this is a goose. Take care of it for me." But instead, he involved humanity in the art of naming.

Naming is both an invitation into co-creation as well as a way to bring order to the immensity of the cosmos. By giving a plant or a person or a desire a name, we take what is nebulous and unfamiliar and give it a shape and personality. Naming changes the relationship. A hurricane is no longer an unknown force out on the ocean, but Hurricane Kathy, a level-four storm that will make landfall by 5 p.m. and dissipate by Tuesday. A hard-shelled insect with protruding horns is no longer a weird mystery of the Amazon, but a Dynastinae, a subfamily of scarab beetles more commonly called the Rhinoceros beetle. The squirming infant the doctor places in your arms is no longer the mystery growing inside you, but Jonah, your son whose warm chocolate eyes pierce right to your soul, just like his daddy's.

Naming takes the unseen, often intangible aspects of our lives and gives them weight, meaning, and purpose. Words give us something to hold on to, and when it comes to belonging, finding words for what is beneath the desire to connect points you in the direction of Love.

Naming in Real Life

"What are you looking for?" These were the first recorded words Jesus spoke in the book of John (John 1:38). Upon noticing two men following him along the road, Jesus turned toward them, and instead of asking "What are you doing?" or "Who are you, and why are you following me?" he moved right past their behavior and dug into their desires. "What are you looking for?" Jesus invited the men to give words to what they wanted, and I believe it is a question he is asking us still. What is beneath our longing? And more specifically, when it comes to our desire to belong, what are you looking for?

We often treat longing like a junk drawer, tossing things in but never really taking time to sort out the rubber bands or the pens that have run out of ink. You ignore the ache, and the longing grows, piling up, until you can no longer shut the drawer. No longer is the desire "out of sight, out of mind," because there it is, demanding attention. There you are alone in a new house in a new city with no one to call. But instead of ignoring the longing until it's spilling out all over the place, what if we learned to take it out and stare at it a bit? What if we embraced habits to answer Jesus' question along the way, "What are you looking for?"

Despite popular belief or commonly held assumptions, our first movement toward belonging is inward. We must become well acquainted with our desires, with who we are and how we are wired and the ways we tend to wobble, because that is where we encounter the image of God inside us—the essence of our original belonging. That is where we remember our worth. By being able to name all the ways we long to give and receive love, belonging moves from being some mysterious, amorphous, intangible idea that is always just out of reach into a welcome already inside us. Naming is an avenue to being known, a way to see the map already within us.

As you move from a posture of lack to one of longing, naming is an important spiritual practice because like Jesus' question, it invites you to look honestly beneath the layers of your yearning and peer into the often-ignored recesses of your soul. By asking yourself, *What am I looking for?* you clear out all the dust and the junk and discover what you have wanted—really wanted—all along. And by giving the desire a name, you learn to hold the longing in your hand and allow what was once a wound to become a place of compassion—no longer a source of shame but a familiar and holy wanting inviting you Home.

The good news is that we do not have to overcomplicate the art of naming. Like good art, naming opens us up to possibility and points to the overlaps in our humanity, but also, good art rarely happens by accident. Rather, artists develop a habit of consistently showing up to the work and having the courage to offer the fullness of who they are and what they have to the world through pen, paint, clay, or song. They recognize that art must be tended, cultivated, and given its proper attention, not once a month or once a year but folded into the fabric of their days. The art of naming is no different. The first step is simply to show up. Whether that's five minutes or five hours, you get to decide. The point is not performance, but carving out time to ask yourself some pointed questions about what you want and giving yourself permission to answer honestly.

For me, naming often looks a little something like this: recently, I set aside time for writing, but when I sat down in the chair, I was caught in a mental fog. The words were not coming (at least, not any decent ones). The blinking cursor ceased to be a friend, hurling insults in my direction. By evening, my emotions had twisted themselves into a tangled mess until I walked away wondering, *Why do I call myself a writer? What if I have run out of words?* (Can you see the lack circling?)

Shame wrapped its tendrils around my work. I could feel the burning in my gut and on my skin, and all I wanted was to douse the ache in a glass of Cabernet. I wanted to throw what I feared was failure into the junk drawer and hope it wouldn't be there tomorrow.

But instead, after the boys were tucked into their beds, I picked up a pen and a journal and let myself explore beneath the self-doubt, beneath the lack, and ask one question until I came to its end: *What is the longing?*

What I found beneath the fear of failure was a need for affirmation.

Ah, yes. That makes sense. Writing is often a solitary sport. The blank page rarely talks back.

However, I remained unsettled. The question begged me to go deeper: *But what is beneath the desire for affirmation?*

Worth, my soul whispered. *I want to know I am wanted, that I have value and my words hold meaning.*

Now we were getting somewhere, because no longer was the blank page about a blank page; it was about the fear that the blank page was a sign of a blank soul.

I circled the words *affirmation* and *worth*. And at the bottom of the page, as the lack slowly melted into longing, I wrote the words: I am not missing anything to be loved.

The entire practice of naming—of assigning words to what I wanted and finding the invitation within—took less than ten minutes. But by deciding to hold the longing in my hand, what I found beneath what I thought was lack was a reminder of who God is and the abundance of his love at my fingertips, and that even in the presence of my inner enemies, I lack nothing. "Only goodness and faithful love will pursue me all the days of my life, and I will dwell in the house of the LORD as long as I live" (Psalm 23:6).

Naming does not heal everything for all time, mind you. I will be back with my pen and journal by tomorrow afternoon, working out my demons. But the art of naming helps us return to the inherent invitation embedded within our longings. Rather than skittering across the surface of our lives, throwing our twistiness into any ol' drawer, we can let Jesus' question "What are you looking for?" lay our desires bare as we actively seek out the invitation on the other side.

Naming and Being Named

Naming is essential to understanding our longings, but naming also reorients us to the wider world. While assigning a name to our desires can keep us from caving in on ourselves beneath the weight of lack, naming also opens the door to let our longing draw us closer to God and then to each other.

Let's go back to the Garden. In the process of naming the creatures, God saw that while the duck-billed platypus and the bobcats were great, they did not satisfy the communal longing inherent in the man. The Divine declared, "It is not good for the man to be alone" (Genesis 2:18). To be honest, that baffles me a little. Adam had full access to God. His presence was not yet complicated by the effects of sin. As an independent introvert (with very loud children), I have to say that Adam's solitary situation sounds pretty great. Sign me up! Yet, despite all that God had declared "good" in his creation, the aloneness of humanity was not one of them. Solitude and isolation are not the same.

When God wove Adam from the dust of the earth and breathed life into his lungs, he declared that unlike the other plants and animals, humankind was crafted in his image. Today, we often think of "image" as what we see when we look into a mirror or our reputation at large. (And if you want to get really cringey, your "personal brand.") But cultural commentators note that "in the ancient world an image was believed to carry the essence of that which it represented." *Image* was a word used to talk about an idol that represented a deity, but it was understood that the image was not a replacement or exact replica of the deity, but an aid in the worship of the deity because "it contained the deity's essence." The original meaning of the word (and its practice) eventually went sideways when "image" became more about man than about God. But when we read about humanity being made and named as an image bearer of the Divine, what that means is that we too carry God's essence, and at its core, the essence of God is communal.

When God looked at Adam, he knew that creating one person in his image was not enough. Inviting that solitary man to co-create and name the creatures alongside him was not enough. Putting a human person in the perfect surroundings was not enough. God said "it is not good" because the fullest representation of his essence required the presence of another image bearer (Genesis 2:18). One person could not reflect God the Father, Son, and Spirit because love cannot exist alone. Humankind is communal because love is the deepest and truest essence of who God is as well as the fullest expression of what it means to be human (1 John 4:7-8).

The end of our longing is God, but we do not find our way alone. By naming, we are reminded that we are named. We are communal reflections of a Divine image and one in whom and with whom God chooses to dwell as we become walking manifestations of his welcome.

That night in Indianapolis, phone in hand, I worked up the courage to direct message a friend of Ben's from high school who I knew lived in the general area. Leslie had been at our wedding, but we had never officially hung out. And while I thought it might be a tad creepy to reach out to a person I knew vicariously through my husband, she was the only person in the city I knew even a little. I tried to play it cool with my message, but felt just as nervous as if I were asking Leslie on a blind date: "Will you be my friend?" Sweaty, I waited for a response.

Leslie was gracious. She responded fairly quickly and invited me to be part of a Bible study. Suddenly, I had not one new friend but six. And while the story could very easily have gone the other way (an unanswered message or a single meetup for coffee that went nowhere), that night became a reminder of how naming our longings is a way for us to avoid caving in on ourselves and turn back out toward God and each other. Through the practice of naming, we can learn to hold our desires for love, safety, affirmation, and respect with open hands, and knowing we are not alone in our need, let it become an arrow pointing us to one another.

Moving Closer

A regular practice of naming our desires can be as simple as pulling out a Post-it note and a pencil and spending five to ten minutes considering: *What do I want?* Go ahead and make an actual list. (I find the tangible act of writing helps me get the ache out of my head so I can see it with my eyes and hold it in my hands.) As you write, pay attention to the longings that surface, and continue to peel back the layers to decipher what core want or desire is beneath the ache. Then, ask yourself: *What does this longing tell me about God, myself, or others? Where do I sense God's invitation?* Go ahead and write it down. You may decide to engage in the art of naming daily, monthly, or as needed, but when you do, take what you find with you, looking for ways you can move toward your desire for deeper connection in the midst of your right-here-right-now life.

8

FROM THEM TO US

If God is my Father, then this is my family.

EUGENE PETERSON

Snow cascaded gently outside the window as Ben and I drove into Bryce Canyon National Park. The weather kept many visitors away that day, giving us a choice of parking spaces in the nearly vacant lot. Stepping out into the cold, a quiet that was both still and wild settled across the land-scape. The small hairs on my arms rose in attention beneath my coat. We walked through evergreens that reached so high we could not see where they ended and the sky began. Snow-covered leaves crunched beneath our feet, and not fifteen feet away, a small herd of deer stood, five sets of bulging eyes watching but not worried enough to disrupt their nibbling. Then, we saw it. The snow and pine needle floor came to an abrupt stop and receded into a deep valley colored by burnt orange clay. The vastness of the canyon was jarring, and I kept a safe distance from the edge. Wind blew hair across my face, yet I could not take my eyes away from the beauty in front of us.

Mile upon mile of openness stood before me. Peeking down into the canyon, curiosity gave way to reverence as I noticed clusters of juniper trees. Bent over like old men, the trees had grown against all odds out of the clay mounds that rose from the canyon like ancient obelisks. No wonder they had named this portion of the canyon "The Cathedral." Ben and I stood silent for several minutes, as if we both understood words would only cheapen the wonder.

But not one hundred yards from where we stood was an outpost, a place where visitors could safely walk out beyond the canyon's edge. Guardrails surrounded the perimeter (for which I was grateful), and every twenty feet or so, telescopes stood mounted along the farthest edge. For a quarter or two, you could squint your eyes, press your face up against the cold metal lens, and zero in on a section of the canyon. How odd those telescopes seemed in the light of day. Amid a backdrop of untamed terrain that seemed to go on and on without end, why would anyone try to contain such beauty? Why look through such a narrow lens?

Sometimes I find God asking me the same when it comes to belonging. Perspective is a tricky thing. No one is to blame for having only two eyes. That is, generally, the number of eyes we are given. Finitude is part of what makes us human, what sets us apart from God himself, but our limited lens on the world, on God, on humanity are also reminders of why we need each other. Two eyes are not enough. Instead, taking the measly quarter out of our hands, he invites us to put down the narrow lens and look out at the wide, wonderful horizon.

Beyond Our Noses

When I first met Sarah, I was certain she had it all figured out. Ben, the boys, and I had recently moved back to Indiana and were trying to make connections within a new church. Sarah and her husband, Cory, sat in the row behind us one Sunday, their family of five (almost six from the look of Sarah's belly) seemed to match the fidgety energy of our own motley crew. We smiled at each other with a knowing that comes from being a bit of a circus everywhere you go.

But something about meeting Sarah stirred up all my latent insecurity. While I affectionately call her "the other Sarah" these days, there's a fair amount of history and truth behind my description. Sarah is many things I am not: tall, vibrant, bold, with cascading blond hair often styled beneath a chic hat. She is all prism and shine, whereas I lean toward an earthier, more muted palette (in fashion but also in life). What stood out to me most when we first met was the air of self-assurance that followed her. I wasn't the only one who noticed. Sarah quickly became known in our church body as a leader, a good thinker, and a gatherer of people, and rightly so. She is all those things. But after that first meeting, as I observed Sarah from the fringes of her life, a bitterness began to churn. Intimidation turned to envy. Longing soured into lack.

I wish I could say I recognized what was happening and took initiative to get over myself and get to know her, but I did not. I kept my distance, hoping the jealousy would wane with time. (It did not.) Sarah reached out first.

She invited me to join her and a few other ladies at a women's conference in Dallas. I had wanted to attend the event for years, so saying yes was easy, but the closer we inched toward leaving, the more I realized I did not know these women well. *What exactly was I getting myself into? Would I spend the whole trip tense and awkward, feeling the internal pressure to be someone I was not?* I could only hold my breath for so long.

The day of the conference arrived, and all six of us loaded into a minivan and set off for the airport. After about twenty minutes on the road, the relational thermostat in the vehicle seemed to shift from awkward to invited. While the weather outside blistered against the van windows, the air inside became alive with the earthiness of spring, warm and welcoming. Stories abounded. The longer we drove and talked, the more the muscles in my shoulders grew lax. A sense of safety increased. My initial instincts toward self-protection gave way to connection as I realized these women carried joys, griefs, and insecurities, just like me.

For the first time, I heard more than tidbits about Sarah's life and the lives of the other women. Stories, new yet familiar, filled the space between us. Tears spilled over in sorrow and in laughter. We found ourselves in the complexity of each other's lives, nodding at narratives of uncertainty in the throes of motherhood, of daring to hold fragile dreams, and of unexpected pain in the wake of loss.

Over the course of the next few days, all the differences I imagined between Sarah and me unraveled like yarn. Yes, our skeins of yarn were very different colors, but beneath all the layers were two women wondering whether they belonged. In all the ways I worried about being "not enough" in the eyes of others, Sarah felt the constant internal critic of being "too much." Beneath her California-girl exterior beat the heart of a woman wondering whether she was really wanted. She questioned: *Am I invited out of obligation? Is my presence really desired at the table? Must I always be "on," or can I just be?*

Despite being a confident, capable leader in our church, Sarah was not immune to feeling out of place. Loneliness lives in both the shadows and the spotlight. Sometimes, the most visible people feel the least seen, the least free to be the fullest version of themselves. I should have known. In many ways, her thoughts mirrored my own, and I found myself mentally erasing so many of the assumptions I once held about her.

On our trip, envy lessened more and more as each day passed, and a friendship with Sarah grew in its place. It was bumpy and awkward for a while, like middle schoolers learning to slow dance. To be honest, our friendship can still be all elbows on occasion, because our personalities are about as different as our appearances. In places where Sarah sees black and white, I see shades of nuance. Sarah is a fast-paced, deep thinker with a strong voice, while I am a big feeler with a slower gait, more content with quiet contemplation and melancholy.

In the midst of all our differences, Sarah has become one of my dearest friends. All the qualities that once caused me angst and envy are now the very things that endear her to me. I celebrate her big hats and flashy skirts, her confident exterior and deep love for theology and God's Word. I cheer her on from my seat when she's leading on stage. While we do not always see eye to eye (both literally and in many figurative ways), we have learned to see and embrace each other with grace and welcoming, just as we are.

It is hard to see the world beyond our own noses, let alone understand all the people and places of the world we have not yet witnessed. While it can be tempting to be content with our single lens, the largeness of God's love invites us to relate differently. His Spirit urges us to see and to love in boundary-pushing, expansive kinds of ways that compel us to move from a picture of "them" to a posture of "us."

The Problem of Sameness

One of the greatest barriers to belonging is our tendency to draw lines around who we are and how we are different. Stanford professor Geoffrey L. Cohen observes, "Our ability to silo ourselves has vastly expanded in the modern era, with online social networks, private schools, and gated communities." One hour on the internet reminds us what can happen when a person steps out of his or her corner. Anger ensues. Assumptions are made. Fury flows freely. Even well-intended discourse can bring out the wolves. We are all prone to looking for our virtuous pound of flesh.

And if we are paying attention, the divides are there, even within ourselves. Out of fear or self-protection or uncertainty or desire for significance, we can easily shrink back from any hint of what seems "other."

Other fashion or music.

Other shades of skin or ways of combing our hair.

Other signs in the front yard.

Other ways of raising a family.

Other views on everything from education to abortion to the Enneagram.

Faced with differences, we become like magnets pulled toward the allure of sameness. We gravitate toward people who are like us. And why not? When we embed our identity within a group, we gain a sense of significance and meaning. Even if we have to shrink or hide ourselves a little, we are willing to bend in order to be accepted by the whole. There's a strange little high that comes with being alike.

Sameness also comes with a measure of safety. From our political views to theological alignment, sexuality to sense of humor, we nestle into our corners, toward people we perceive to be like us, because sameness can be both comforting and familiar. The original motivation for these securities comes from somewhere good—a desire for Home. But by cozying up in our neat and tidy corners, we inadvertently and often subconsciously create a culture of "us" and "them," further perpetuating the divides that increase our feelings of loneliness, isolation, and exclusion. We feel safe—but only for a season or in certain places. Only if we can stay within the group.

But imagine what the world would be like if we were all the same. Same personality. Same jokes. Same recipes. Same color of eyes or set of beliefs. That kind of sameness within our families, let alone the world, sounds straight-up boring (if not a tad creepy). I certainly would not want to spend the rest of my life with a carbon copy of myself. I am not so sure we would make it!

The threat of monotony is one thing, but if we look at the life of Jesus, we can see that sameness is not a value of the kingdom. Jesus broke all kinds of societal structures when he chose to be with people unlike himself: blind beggars, tax collectors, women, and a litany of other people who had been ostracized or pushed to the margins. The disciples themselves were a scraggly, dissimilar group of guys who constantly bickered over their perceived differences and jockeyed for position. And what did Jesus do when they asked, "Who is the greatest?" He did not find a new group of dudes or point to one of them and say, "Him. He's the best. Do what he does." Instead, Jesus invited a small child to stand next to him, looked the disciples in the eyes, and said, "Whoever welcomes this little child in my name welcomes me. And whoever welcomes me welcomes him who sent me. For whoever is least among you—this one is great" (Luke 9:46-48).

The gospel has never been a call to sameness, but to Jesus. And when we forget that, when we do not embrace that "we who are many are one body in Christ" and Christ alone, we grasp for sameness in an attempt to find confirmation that we are right, that we are in fact the greatest.

That is the problem with sameness. Instead of learning to live and love alongside people who are different (and perhaps quite difficult), we posture ourselves in places of self-appointed virtue rather than welcome. Like the older brother, we see ourselves as better and lose sight of our common need, the shared humanity that runs through us all.

Looking again at that story of Jesus and his disciples, it's laughable, really, that Jesus chose a child to illustrate a posture of welcome. I don't know if you've ever tried to do a normal task like cooking or laundry with a kid lately, but it makes everything harder, longer, and twice as messy. I have lost track of the number of times I have cringed as my youngest poured flour across the kitchen island while helping me bake cookies. So I think it is no small detail that Jesus pulled a child next to him as he responded to their question about greatness. It is as if he is telling us, "A life of welcome is not going to be easy. It's going to get messy and winding and full of frustration at times. You are going to want to go back to doing it yourself. But here in the eyes of a child, in the gaze of one who is not inclined to do things your way, you will find me. Here you will learn what it really means to be great."

The shift from them to us is not an easy one, because many of our differences will not disappear. Nor should they. Unity is not uniformity, and taking a posture of welcome means we do not hide or deny all the brilliant complexities embodied within a person. Rather, we make room for them. We bravely bring our whole selves into the room and invite others to do the same, knowing there are no heroes in this story, only people. We are a tapestry of vibrant, crusty, questioning, confident, loud, enigmatic, energetic, exhausted people all woven from the same cloth. There is no them. There is only us.

The more we push back against the seduction of sameness, the more we begin to see that beauty. The more we celebrate our differences, the more we can learn from the ways other people experience the world. The more we widen our gaze, the more our souls soften toward people we once kept at a distance as we catch a glimpse of ourselves in each other and witness the vastness of a good and creative God.

Who Is Them?

Most of us do not like to think about the ways we might be inadvertently diminishing the humanity of others. Shoulder muscles tense. The jaw becomes rigid. Fists clench, as if we are subconsciously ready for a fight. We do not like to be confronted with the ugliness of how we elevate ourselves, even if it happens within the unseen places of our hearts and minds. Confronting bias can be like seeing your face in one of those oversized mirrors that reveal everything down to the pores. Who wants to be seen in such microscopic ways? Not me. I'll take my windowless, poorly lit bathroom, thank you very much.

But one thing I have discovered about life with God is that love does not like to leave us in the dark. The sun always rises beyond our backyard, revealing all that transpired during the night. The morning reveals our secrets, but it also glows gold with mercy. We do not have to be afraid of what we might find lurking in our own shadows. We do not have to be leery of what we might find as we step into the light.

Expanse requires exposure. The ways we subtly categorize "them" and "us" often hide and may not be visible without a little effort. Most of us carry preconceived ideas about people that lurk in our subconscious, remain unchallenged by our insular families, or are cloaked beneath the guise of good. But like the rhythm of spring cleaning, we can make regular room inside ourselves for each other by setting aside time for some honest reflection as we contemplate a few simple (but hard) questions:

Who is "them"?

Who do you tend to avoid?

Whose opinion makes your eyes roll?

Where do you harbor a sense of superiority or knowing-better-than?

Are there people or cultures that make you uncomfortable?

Do you have family members or people in your church small group or book club that cause you to grit your teeth every time you get together?

These questions are difficult. Personal. Revealing. Often, the longer we sit with them, the longer the parade of people passes through our minds. The names and faces vary for each of us, and they may not automatically reveal a hidden bias, the belief that you are "more" in one way or another. But those names and faces are worth paying attention to. They are worth pulling out the magnified mirror to get honest about what we think, feel, and believe about those individuals and how we see them in relation to ourselves. Because when we shine a light on how we see each other, we realize that there are many more of "them" within us than we realized. But there is also much more room for us.

The good (yet still hard) news is this: The more we move into the light, the more clearly we see our posture toward other people. The more we practice paying attention to the opening and closing of our souls or the places where bitterness creeps in, the more we can know the people with whom we can grow in compassion. The more we know the dark and dusty corners of our souls, the more we can whisper into the darkness, "Create in me a clean heart, O God"

(Psalm 51:10 KJV). And he hears us. He takes us back to the beginning where we can dig our fingers down into the common dirt from which we came, where we can find the rich and abundant soil of our shared humanity. In the warmth of the summer sun, the Father breathes life into us once again as he restores our vision for what was and is and is yet to be, both in and among us. He sets our feet on common ground and points us toward each other.

I understand it is scary to confront our narrowness and be stretched to see the world beyond our own eyes. Standing on the precipice rarely feels safe. One slip of the foot or strong wind causes even adrenaline junkies like my husband to take a step back, because we realize just how vulnerable we are against the elements. We become painfully aware of our limitations when pitted against the unpredictability of creation. The earth is wild—and so are people. The fear of falling is real.

But by choosing to step up to the edge and turn our heads from side to side, we begin to see the chasms we create between us and find ways to move a little closer. We erase the lines we once drew around ourselves and become people committed to an infinite and eternal lens. Day by day, inch by inch, person by person, we learn to see and to love a little wider.

Looking Inward

Moving from a posture of "them" to "us" requires an awareness of the ways we might be elevating ourselves over other people, and while that realization is essential, the reality can be hard to hold. I suggest finding a quiet place where you can spend some time with the question *Who is 'them'?* Reread the list of questions on page 85. As you go through each one, let names and faces pass through your mind. Then, ask God to help you reorient yourself to see each person as equal and loved. In these moments I often utter a simple prayer: *God, forgive me for thinking I am better. Help me to see each person like you do, for they are no less loved.* The prayer is not magic. Use your own words or sit in silence if that's better. But let God sit with you in that moment, asking him to help you relate from a place of deeper, more expansive love.

9

THE STORIES BETWEEN US

Could a greater miracle take place than for us
to look through each other's eyes for an instant?

HENRY DAVID THOREAU

It had been a few weeks since I had seen Daniel. Over the holidays, I noticed he was not at his usual spot on the corner of Coventry and Jefferson, and whenever a week, then two weeks, passed without seeing Daniel I began to worry. I wondered whether I would ever see him again.

The last time I had talked with Daniel, just before Christmas, he told me he was bunking with someone, but the situation was not good.

"I gotta get out of there," he said. "Get my own place. I'm just tryna pull together the money."

I did not press him, but I could see the hint of desperation, maybe even a flicker of fear, in his eyes. So when I did not see Daniel for nearly a month, I had reason to worry.

Then, on January 9, there was Daniel. A long exhale containing the silent worry I had been carrying exited my lungs as I parked my truck near his corner. When he saw me coming, his eyes lit up and his mouth curved upward in delight. He put down his sign made from the top of a red plastic bin and hobbled closer, saying, "Hey! How are ya?"

Daniel extended his arms, and we hugged. I tried to remember how long it had been since hugging had become part of what we do, since we had morphed from strangers who occasionally exchanged a few bucks to people who knew a handful of details about each other's lives. To people who hugged.

"I got the place!" he said, near giddy with excitement. Relief loosened the muscles that ran from the back of my ears to the edge of my shoulders, and from the lightness in his eyes, I could see he felt it too. We hugged again.

"God is good!" he said, raising his arms a little higher in the air.

Daniel repeats this phrase often, and while every time I respond with some version of "yes he is!" my eyes narrow a little as I wonder whether he really means it. Maybe I am wondering whether I do too.

He asked about the kids, and I proceeded to tell him that the boys were back in school after the holiday break. "I think it's good for all of us," I said. He nodded knowingly but with a laugh, and I returned his smile.

The light at the intersection near us turned from red to green, and a man's hand reached out through the passenger-side window of a red sedan, handing Daniel a little cash as he went by. I knew that this was my cue to leave. Every minute he stood talking with me, dozens of cars passed by, each one a missed opportunity, so I never stayed long. I never wanted to be the reason he didn't make rent.

"I better get going," I told him, but as I turned, he yelled after me, "Hey! You sure you're okay?"

Another breath escaped my lips, but this time, the air felt fragile. Tears gathered in the corners of my eyes.

"I'm tired, Daniel," I said with a half-smile, his warmth melting away any self-righteousness I had carried with me to the corner that day.

"Okay, yeah, I thought there was somethin'."

I don't know whether it was the cold Indiana wind or the kindness that emanated from Daniel's gaze, but a shiver ran through me as I whispered, "Thank you." And I meant it. In the deepest parts of me, I was grateful to be seen by him, for my weariness to be recognized and compassion held out before me.

The green light turned to red. A new batch of cars were bumper to bumper in all three lanes, so I wrapped my sweater around me a little tighter and waved goodbye. Daniel turned toward the street and held up his sign, and as I stepped up into my truck, I heard his voice lift over the sound of the wind and traffic, "God is good!"

Tales That Hurt

The threads that weave between us as human people are not always evident. So much of our lives are spent on the surface, moving from one place to another without stopping to reflect on how we relate, that we often fail to recognize the ways we distance ourselves from people we perceive to be different. We may not realize that our hearts are postured toward certain narratives—the stories we believe about each other before we have exchanged a single word.

One of the most central things about being human is how we lean toward a well-told tale. We get up in the morning, mentally rehearsing conversations that have not yet taken place. At lunch, we munch quietly on burritos while inconspicuously listening to coworkers talk about a recent shopping trip to T.J. Maxx. We glance at the man revving the engine of his dirt-covered pickup truck in the next lane, and after two seconds of eye contact, already we have developed a tale of who he is and where he is going. (My guess is that even now, you have an image of that man in your mind. Go ahead. Say hello to him for me.)

All day long, we live in a web of story. And one of the most amazing things about stories is how, like moths circling a lantern on a July night, we cannot resist the urge to move closer. As Jonathan Gottschall writes, "Human minds yield helplessly to the suction of story." Yet, stories can also get the better of us.

My guess is that most of us don't set out to develop us-versus-them mentalities. We do not intentionally push people into corners or categories out of avarice or a desire to harm, either literally or in our minds. While I am sure it happens, most parents do not sit their kids down for a lesson on "who we hate" or "why we are better." And if we compare ourselves to the divisive extremes we see within our wider culture, we can convince ourselves that we are doing quite well. Pitted against wars fought in the name of politics, theology, ethnicity, gender, sexuality (the list goes on), our day-to-day interactions and behaviors seem pretty vanilla. Good, even.

But that's the sneaky thing about bias: it is always there, lurking beneath the floorboards of how we relate. Social scientists have a name for these innate responses, how bias manifests itself in internal narratives that often go unnoticed in the hustle and bustle of life. They call it the *fundamental attribution error* (or FAE, for short). The basic principle of FAE is that all of us have a set of default perspectives and responses (based on a complex culmination of personality, experience, culture, family of origin), and when we are in situations with clear gaps of knowledge or understanding, each of us has a tendency to fall back into our biases, into the default stories we believe beneath our skin.

The most damaging aspect of these types of tales, especially in relation to belonging, is that our defaults can be incredibly binary (this or that, black or white, us or them). Our snap reactions often do not account for the situation at large and can lead us to believe that observed behaviors are indicative of a person's character or personhood rather than a product of a complex situation.

Imagine with me for a moment: you're in a hurry at the grocery store because you're late getting home. All you need is milk. But as you make your way to the dairy section, a middle-aged man stops directly in front of you. His cart completely blocks your path. You stand there silently, impatience growing. A few seconds turns into thirty, and as your frustration escalates, your FAE kicks in and begins to tell you a story about the man: "What a self-centered moron! Surely he sees me out of the corner of his eye. Who can be this socially unaware . . . or uncaring?!" The man eventually moves without much of an apology, and you reach for the milk as a string of salty words passes through your mind.

We've all been in these types of situations. At the grocery store. On the interstate. In the school pickup line. We perceive the other person's behavior in a negative light, and instead of trying to expand our lens on the story and make room for the situation, we make assumptions about the person's character.

"What a jerk."

"He is so simple-minded."

"She's so self-consumed."

But people who have studied the complexities of human behavior and belonging warn us against such snap judgments, reminding us that quick assumption "leaves little room in our minds to imagine the complexities and contradictions of people." Each of us is more than one thing, moment, or behavior. That man at the grocery store might have just received a bad diagnosis. Maybe he had really poor eyesight or social anxiety. Perhaps he was wanting to pick out just the right milk to take home to his kids, who he rarely saw but were in town for the weekend. It's very likely his actions had nothing to do with you at all. There was a larger situation at play.

But without becoming familiar with our biases—the stories we tell ourselves as we interact with one another—and being willing to name them, even our "good" deeds can spring from the unspoken belief that we are better than the person on the other side.

I began stopping at Daniel's corner to give him a few bucks and a couple cheeseburgers from the McDonald's down the street. While stirred by compassion (a good motivator), a measure of superiority lurked beneath my actions. I left feeling like the hero, thus confirming my sense of virtue. But the reality I have uncovered after a few years of five-minute sidewalk conversations is that Daniel and I are much more the same than I originally wanted to believe. We both have needs. While Daniel stands on a street corner, certain needs a little more evident because of his prosthetic limbs and plastic red sign, we carry the same desire for someone to know our names, ask "how are you?" and listen with genuine care. If I had stuck with my default story, I would have never been able to see the overlaps between us, how we are both looking for a place to call Home.

Tales That Heal

While our default stories can be a source of misunderstanding and hurt, narrative can also be an avenue of healing. In my relationships with both Sarah and Daniel, while very different from one another, our sense of connectedness was not built on an alignment of values or skin color or shared interests, but on bearing witness to each other's stories. Little by little. Piece by piece. It's what ties us together still.

Because even amid great differences, stories weave us together. They pave a path to belonging where knowledge, skill set, and personality fall short. In telling others of our childhood wounds, broken hearts, fears, joys, and failures, we see beyond the surface of our lives and catch a glimpse of a soul not unlike our own. A little light breaks through, drowning out the echoes of our loneliness and linking us to something much larger. Stories reveal our shared humanity, and in that commonality, we find healing.

The overlap we experience in telling and listening to each other's stories is no small thing. We experience the connection not only in our minds and emotions but also in our bodies. Psychiatrist Curt Thompson writes, "When a person tells her story and is truly heard and understood, both she and the listener undergo actual changes in their brain circuitry. They feel a greater sense of emotional and relational connection, decreased anxiety, and greater awareness of and compassion for others' suffering." Even if only for a moment, story allows us to peek through each other's eyes. Here we find increased understanding and the realization that the desire to belong flows in and through us all.

It's no wonder Jesus himself spoke so often in stories, in earthly parables that peeled back the layers of eternity. It was as if he knew that in the face of cultural differences, economic gaps, religious piety, and oppression, story alone would be our common language. Tales of rich men unable to pry their fingers off their wealth, of widows donating their last cent, and of lost sons trying to find their way home became the foundation for a different way of relating not only to God but also to each other. So I wonder: For the sake of our belonging, what if we give in? What if we let story become the gravity that pulls us together rather than the wedge that drives us apart?

I think what we will find is that stories widen our lens if we will let them. The more we seek out each other's stories rather than filling in the gaps with unexamined assumptions, the more we can discover the beauty of maintaining our differences while letting down our guards. Because in the light of story, "them" fades to "us." Through story, we hear echoes of ourselves in each other as we realize the need for love, acceptance, safety, food in our bellies, and a roof over our heads runs through us all. Empathy rises within us as we discover the same joys that get us out of bed and the same sorrows that make us climb back beneath the covers. Story reveals how we both wrestle with anger or how Friday nights often leave us lonely. Even when we are wounded, story helps us recognize the "complexities and contradictions" of what it means to be human and maintain a tender heart.

I don't know what will become of my friendship with Daniel. Once again, it's been a couple weeks since I've seen him at his corner, and I'm beginning to wonder how he is and what has become of him. But that does not change the fact that knowing Daniel in small, ordinary ways has softened the way I see people as I go throughout my day. Our conversations have planted seeds of compassion where judgment once lived. Through Daniel, God has grown in me a more grounded view of human people and shown me all the ways love still needs room to grow inside me.

The practice of seeking out the stories between us does not come without risk. It takes courage, perseverance, and humility to see the world with eyes other than our own, and what we find may not always be pretty. We may not like the default tales we see within ourselves or know how to hold the complexities of the other person, leaving us without a clear-cut path to navigate the nuance. But if we are "to grasp how wide and long and high and deep is the love of Christ, and to know this love that surpasses knowledge," we can let our stories open us up "to the measure of all the fullness of God" (Ephesians 3:18-19 NIV). As people of welcome, we can let them move us out of our huddles of sameness toward a less-uniform way of seeing the world.

Yes, stories will stretch us. Our souls, our minds, our bodies will be taken to their limits, because that's how much God loves us. Like a mother growing new life in her womb, love expands. It tests the confines of our skin and forms us, and while the growth can be awkward, uncomfortable, and straight-up painful at times, there is freedom and abundance in the silver streaks that run like tattoos across our skin, because these are stretch marks worth bearing.

Moving Closer

Seeking out the stories of others helps us slow down our assumptions and grow our compassion. Certainly, we want to know the stories of the people in our face-to-face lives. But another simple way we can engage with story is through books or movies that depict experiences, cultures, or perspectives different from our own. As we read or watch, we can pay attention to our internal responses and tap into our imaginations, stepping inside that person's experience and allowing God to grow our empathy and understanding.

10

FROM CERTAIN TO SETTLED

> doesn't it get tiresome, telling
> people how to live? give me
> it up—tell me a tale:
> words to live by.

C. RAYNOR

"Mom, I have a question."

We had been sitting in the dark for several minutes. I was near enough to my son's bed to hear his long, deep breathing. I thought he had fallen asleep or was at least close to it, but I was wrong, evidenced by the small voice that cut through the night.

"Okay, bud. What's your question?"

"Well," he paused with a punctuated sigh, "I just wonder what God looks like."

"Mmmmm. Yes. I wonder that too. What do you think he looks like?"

Another sigh. "Well, when I close my eyes and think about God, I see the color yellow."

A smile spread across my face. I had never thought about God as color, how he might reveal himself to us like a kaleidoscope. "I like that, buddy."

"What is heaven like, Mom?"

It was my turn to sigh. I paused, as all the images I had gathered from Sunday school lessons and sermons passed through my mind. A swell of emotion surged through my chest, as I thought about the inexplicable tie I have felt to the afterlife since Carter's passing. His death seemed to make life beyond our temporal bodies a little more accessible, but I too carried my questions, so I paused. I recognized the rising internal pressure to give my son answers as we sat together in the darkness, but all I could offer him in that moment was the truth: "I don't know for sure. It's hard to say since I've never been there. But I think we get to be with God and each other in ways we haven't been before, without stuff like pain or brokenness coming between us. What do you think?"

The conversation continued a little longer, each of us trading ideas, and while we did not arrive at concrete conclusions, a satisfied quiet settled in the room. Sleep was near. But before we said our final goodnights, I wanted him to know, "J, you ask really good questions."

"Thanks, Mom." I could hear his toothy grin as he settled further into bed and pulled the comforter up around his chin.

For a few more minutes, I stayed next to him, watching his chest rise and fall by the gentle glow of a Buzz Lightyear night-light. My mind circled a few more times around our conversation, his questions inviting me to ask God my own. Again, no answers emerged out of the darkness, and yet, as I pulled my body off the bedroom floor, I could not help but be rocked by a gentle sense of being known.

Experts and Answers

We all need a steady place to plant our feet, and questions are often an attempt at finding our footing as we reach out to one another. From infancy, human flourishing depends on our ability to develop healthy, secure attachments—a style of relating that sees oneself as "worthy of love" and others as "generally accepting and responsive." Psychiatrist Curt Thompson observes that "virtually every action we humans take is part of the deeper attempt to connect with other humans." We want to know that if we reach out, someone will be there to reach back.

However, when it comes to developing secure attachments, what is perhaps more important than providing easy, digestible answers is a willingness to be present with one another. Yes, we want remedies or solutions or resolve, but even more than that, we want to know that we can whisper our questions into the darkness and the person listening will stay. That even if we shrug our shoulders at mysteries beyond us both, at least we still have each other.

But sitting together with our questions is not a common occurrence in our highly individualized, Google-happy, self-help Westernized lives. We would much rather find a five-step program than sit alone in the unknown. We want something to do, because letting questions go unanswered often leaves us with a wave of nauseating discomfort and a reminder we are far from being in control.

Perhaps these cultural norms combined with the need for secure attachment is why we are so quick to move toward experts and answers. We do not have to look long or far to notice that our world elevates the loud and the flashy, the self-assured prophet full of certainty. We become wooed by individuals with big personalities and shiny ideas and get behind leaders with puffed-up attitudes, despite the people they may have trampled along the way. We applaud outcomes without asking questions about the means. We award quantity over quality and measure following instead of faithfulness. To top it all off, we too seek to become experts—to be known for what we know (or at least the appearance of it).

The ancient church at Thessalonica seemed to have a similar problem. Perfectly situated for commerce along major trade routes, the city of first-century Thessalonica became a target for the power-hungry Roman Empire. The church there dealt not only with a consumeristic, merchant-based culture but also with the greed and hate of the Roman Empire. But in the apostle Paul's letter to the Thessalonian church, he urged Christ followers there to "seek to lead a quiet life, to mind your own business, and to work with your own hands" (1 Thessalonians 4:11). Perhaps the Thessalonian church wanted to beat the Romans at their own game or, at least, to catch their attention. But, in the face of greed and authoritarianism, Paul encouraged the church to prioritize a different set of values as a way to love well, reminding them not to confuse noise with knowing and self-importance with substance. Perhaps we need that reminder as well.

The more fine lines emerge around the corners of my eyes and the complexity of life blurs black and white into gray, I have come to realize there is a difference between being certain and being settled. Certainty plants its feet in concrete. It prides itself in fast answers and allows no room for movement. No way to bend or flex or grow. Differences are often viewed as threats to be diminished, unwanted weeds poking out of the cement, and instead of approaching these variations as human people made in the image of God, certainty elevates itself above the other and casts shadows upon those who think, believe, or live differently.

But we can be settled without being certain. Rooted in humility, the settled are steady but soft. Their curious feet are on the ground but still moving. Still seeking. Still looking up into the sky or in the face of a baby and acknowledging the vast mystery of God. Like David, whose own heart beat in cadence with the Creator, the settled move toward the love of the Father and proclaim, "This wondrous knowledge is beyond me. It is lofty; I am unable to reach it" (Psalm 139:6; see also 1 Samuel 13:14). While the certain posture themselves as experts, the settled value knowledge as a way to wisdom and compassion, a path to welcome rather than a weapon to wield against one another. As people of welcome, we can be steadied by the abiding love of God but still ask our questions. We can dare to shrug our shoulders and say to one another, "I don't know."

The Land of I Don't Know

Recently, I pulled an old journal off a shelf and began flipping through the pages. I do not know what I was looking for exactly, but what I found was a snapshot of me two years ago. I remember that woman and her struggle to talk with God, how old ways of praying weren't working. Instead, my words found their way to the Father through poems written in the early morning hours. Those poems had been a lifeline, and as I swept fingers over page after page of words no one else would ever see, I was haunted by the ghosts of not only who I once was but also who I was becoming. My chest swelled with compassion and gratitude for my younger self, as the words of poet John Blase returned to me, "It's all essential."

At any given moment, we don't know what we don't know. Our personhood builds and grows. We are never static. As James K. A. Smith observes, we are like waves, guided by a past, cresting in the present, while always moving toward a future. We are forever shifting. As we make our way in the world, we become gatherers of information, ideas, experiences, and stories. While we may not be able to see the vastness of the shore in any one moment, we can hold the essentialism of all that we have collected and leave room for all that is yet to unfold, in ourselves and in each other. We can be settled while still living in The Land of I Don't Know.

To be settled is to be humble—to be people of *humus*, of the earth. Grounded, but growing. Yes, humility might require us to sit down in the dirt, but humility is neither a lack of confidence in who we are nor a diminishment of our gifts, abilities, and beliefs. Rather, humility is knowing and accepting ourselves as we are (the good, the bad, and the cringeworthy) while remaining open to the perspectives and the people around us. To be humble is to embrace the idea that everyone is a person in process, constantly in a state of becoming. Just as you are not the same person you were five years ago, you are not the person you will be in another five, ten, or twenty years down the road. Humility encourages your evolving humanity without diminishing the person you are right now. It's all essential.

Social psychologist Daryl Van Tongeren, who spent years researching and exploring the effects of humility on cultures, writes, "True, authentic humility is a secure openness to the world, where we can be honest with ourselves and others about our strengths and limitations, seeking to learn new perspectives and caring deeply about those around us." I love that phrase: *secure openness*. The words convey both confidence and hospitality, authenticity and grace, finitude and freedom. In humility, we do not have to change who we are or have everything figured out in order to be worthy of knowing, because we recognize we are human people like everyone else. Not heightened experts but fellow pilgrims.

Yet humility is more than a vessel of self-settledness meant to produce inner peace. What Van Tongeren's years of research also revealed is that humility is a posture that moves us toward each other. He notes, "Humility is a way of approaching ourselves, other people, and the world around us with a sense of enough-ness, an unconditional worth and value that opens us to the world as it is." Humility expands our welcome. It is the deep breath that fills our lungs, allowing us to exhale as we stand a little straighter in our skin and reach out to God and each other. Humility is secure attachment in action.

If belonging were a home in The Land of I Don't Know, then humility is the fragrance that invites us to settle in. Being with a humble person is like cozying down into a comfortable couch, a space where you can take off your shoes and stay awhile. Their gentle authenticity invites you to come near, bring your whole self into the room, ask your questions, and embrace your own personal brand of weirdness. Their willingness to admit when they are wrong or confess their not-knowing becomes an open door for others to do the same. Humility holds our questions.

The more settled we become, the more we begin to see ourselves for who we are and develop a contentedness with how we fit into the greater whole—with God, our families, our friendships, and the wider world. We can enter a room and instead of trying to be the expert or mold ourselves to become more or less, we can see with clear, kind, and curious eyes how we belong. We can come into the room knowing we are already worthy to be there, and without the pressure to find acceptance, we become free to invite others, "Come sit! And bring your questions."

Unlikely Vessels

It is often easier to be an expert than a question-asker. We develop a false sense of security in our certainty, because appearances and opinions are easier to maintain at a distance. No one can see our flaws and uncertainties if they're kept far off because, as John Mark Comer observes, "Community exposes what's inside of you."

But community also keeps us steady as we actively learn what it means to "do nothing out of selfish ambition or conceit, but in humility consider others as more important than yourselves" (Philippians 2:3). Perhaps that is one of the reasons Jesus surrounded himself with his disciples. Having been shown the "the kingdoms of the world and their splendor" in the wilderness and made acutely aware of the temptation of power and greatness, maybe Jesus knew he needed to be surrounded by people who kept him grounded. He did not need to have good connections or places of influence, but friends who would walk alongside him on dusty roads. He needed companions who would bear witness to his own suffering and stick around even when what he said made no earthly sense.

I think about the night before his arrest when Jesus went into the garden to pray, but he did not go alone. He could have easily let his disciples think he was not afraid or anxious and slip away by himself unnoticed so that when the time came he could put on a brave face. Instead, Jesus asked Peter, James, and John to come with him into Gethsemane, revealing to them, "I am deeply grieved to the point of death. Remain here and stay awake with me" (Matthew 26:36-46).

The humility of Jesus in this moment is astounding. I think of all the times I have hid in my bedroom closet when I needed an ugly cry, only to emerge when I felt like I had collected myself and the pain was no longer evident on my puffy, red face. But here is Jesus, seeing himself in that moment for who he was—afraid and full of sorrow—and yet asking his closest friends to come near. He did not try to be more or less than what he was. With all the knowledge of eternity at his fingertips, Jesus chose humility to be the unlikely vessel for his humanity.

Everything inside me wanted to give my son a textbook answer to his questions about heaven or (in the least) regurgitate the flannelgraph lessons I had been given. Perhaps it was pride. Perhaps it was the desire to give my son something, anything to hold on to. Likely, it was a bit of both. But sitting in his bedroom that night, I chose to say the words "I don't know" both because it was honest and because I wanted our son to see what it looked like to be people of *humus*, to sit down and ask questions and fathom the mystery of being human, which tells us:

You do not have to know to be known.

You do not have to be certain to be settled.

You can hold your questions without answers, because even here in the dirt you are held.

Looking Inward

Similar to how we name our longings, we can name our questions. In doing so, we become more comfortable cupping our uncertainties in the palms of our hands. One simple way to do just that is to ask, *What questions am I holding?* Then, we can list or acknowledge the questions. We do not have to hypothesize answers or explain why we are asking that particular question. Rather, by naming the questions, we give ourselves permission to say "I don't know" and move from being certain to being settled.

11

SAY THE QUESTIONS

> Mystery surrounds every deep experience
> of the human heart: the deeper we go into
> the heart's darkness or its light, the closer we get
> to the ultimate mystery of God.

PARKER PALMER

A wall of stained-glass windows lined the back half of the sanctuary. I grew up in a Baptist church on the outskirts of a rural town, and while thoroughly evangelical, the building retained vestiges of its liturgical beginnings. Formerly St. Anthony Novitiate, the expansive grounds had once been a place of training for Catholic priests, and the stained glass was one of the many ways their sacred traditions seemed to have worked their way into the walls. As kids, we loved to explore the building, ducking into maintenance hallways and down back stairwells, telling each other stories of the monks who once walked there. (We Baptist kids did not know the difference between friars and monks, priests and pastors, so the actual history got a little lost in translation, muddied by time, hushed whispers, and bustling imaginations.)

"The building has secret tunnels," my friend Christa once told me. Our eyes grew wide at the possibilities of what lurked beneath the sanctuary. We did our best to find the passageways, taking advantage of youth group lock-ins to do a little exploring. We became experts at jimmying the lock to the sanctuary's large wooden doors using a credit card and a little finesse. But despite how many times we investigated beneath the baptismal, in janitor's closets, or in the dusty corners of the furnace room, we never found the tunnels or any signs of them. Perhaps they were never there. Maybe the stained-glass windows had simply whet our appetites for mystery, enlarging our spiritual imaginations beyond weekly Bible verse memory and plastic cup Communion.

Curiosity was not a word I heard in reference to the Christian life until my late twenties. Instead, spiritual conversations were peppered with words like *discipline*, *devotions*, and *outreach*— words that emphasized doing. While nothing is inherently wrong with these words, I found myself struggling to reconcile my inner life with outward expectations and expressions of my faith. Performance seemed to overshadow presence, and the mystery of God felt more like a problem to solve than a greatness to behold. Yet I was drawn toward those stained-glass windows. I was compelled by the red, orange, and green hues that painted row after row of chairs, and I was deeply aware of how urgency seemed to melt off my shoulders as I sat within their light.

Looking back, I think I was always a contemplative soul in an evangelical world. But what I did not realize is that in all those hours I spent staring at the stained glass, getting lost in my thoughts, or hiding in my bedroom to compose songs or craft poems (poems I am glad have gone missing with time), I was learning to peel back the layers of my inner land-scape and pay attention to where the light of God emerged. I was learning to make room for mystery and lean into the questions that arose within me. Without realizing it, I was practicing curiosity.

When we allow space to linger in what we do not know, we participate in a type of divine noticing that invites us to ask our questions. Like finding small stones in a rushing river, we pick our queries up out of the water and hold them. We feel the coolness against our skin and familiarize ourselves with the contours. We make friends with what has been lingering still and silent beneath the rush. And as we grow in courage, we pass them around, feeling the weight of one another's ques-tions against our fingertips. While the rocks may not give rise to answers like a Magic 8 Ball, through shared curiosity, we learn to be together with our questions as we sense the gentle invitation of the Spirit, "Be still, and know that I am God" (Psalm 46:10 ESV).

A Shared Curiosity

Mystery welcomes us to pay attention to our questions, but curiosity invites us to follow them. Holding the unsolved mys-teries of our church building, it was not enough for me to sit silently in the sanctuary and imagine what life might have been like for those priests-in-training. Like yeast left to rise, my ques-tions ballooned into full-blown curiosity. I was no longer content to hold my wonderings; I wanted to go exploring. I wanted, as Rainer Maria Rilke wrote, to "live the questions" and the freedom to say them out loud.

As children, we practice curiosity with a little more ease. We have a question, so we ask it. It doesn't matter if the time is right or who is around; without hesitation we fling our questions out into the cosmos. And usually, kids are not looking for in-depth answers. Our boys are often more content the fewer words we use. Their eyes glaze over the moment a response becomes a soliloquy or (heaven forbid) a sermon. Most of the time, they aren't looking for all the details, not really; they just want a little something to hold and to know that they have been heard.

But my favorite moments are when I do not have an answer and their little eyes light up, "Let's search it up, Mom!" We pull out my laptop and together start exploring:

How far away is Jupiter?

What does a real hedgehog look like?

When was Super Mario Bros. made?

Nestled into the loveseat, we pursue the question side by side, equally eager to discover where it takes us. And I think that is curiosity's sweet spot. When we find others to invite into the journey, curiosity is no longer a lonesome road, but an adventure. Our shared questions provide solidarity and build trust. No longer bound by certainty, we settle a little further into our skin and scoot closer to one another by saying the questions out loud. Without pressure to provide answers, we let mystery lead us further into our belonging, trusting, as Lore Ferguson Wilbert writes, that "God created you curious because he wants to be found." And he wants us to find him in and alongside each other, as curiosity fosters communion.

The Open Door

Moving from certain to settled in a posture of humility does not just happen, but at the same time, it can be difficult to manufacture. The moment we think we have humility mastered, we are likely to have found ourselves right back at the beginning. Trying to avoid being "wise in your own estimation" turns out to be more difficult than we like (Romans 12:16).

I have a lot of natural know-it-all inside me. Maybe it's a firstborn thing. Maybe it's tied to my personality. Maybe it's my long-standing struggle with wanting to trade being known for being seen. It's probably a little of all of that. But for many years, that readiness to give an answer was a barrier between me and my sister Laura.

Nine years separate the two of us. Back when we both lived at home, our mutual big feelings and my tendency to mother her were often a volatile combination. Eyes rolled. Tears were shed. Teeth clenched in fury. I can still see the fire in Laura's eyes the day I accidentally cut her hair too short, after I insisted I knew what I was doing. (I didn't.) And while I did not admit my error that day, I watched Laura look at herself tearfully in the mirror and knew my certainty had led us both into trouble. My confidence had ruined not only my sister's beautiful head of hair (at least, for a few weeks) but also our trust.

But adulthood has softened us both. Earlier this spring, Laura and I took a road trip—a full forty-eight hours of uninterrupted, kid-free time. Just us. The words flowed freely. We talked about everything and anything, but not as older sister and younger sister. We talked as friends and confidants. We gave each other room to speak the questions and linger in the gray space together.

It was that weekend, as we ate chicken salad and settled into the high-backed wooden booth at a quaint country café, that I realized how far we had come. The more Laura and I have let ourselves be human with each other, the more the old power dynamics have slipped away. The more we have voiced our uncertainties, the more surety has been replaced by safety, competition has faded into friendship, and curiosity has become our common language. Our deepening friendship has been one of the best and unexpected gifts of the last decade, and I know the story would have been different if I had never put aside my know-it-all-ness that kept getting in the way.

Because while certainty shuts the door, curiosity props it open. We may not know where our questions will lead us, what we will find on the other side, because mystery is mystery for a reason. But by keeping the door open, we position ourselves in welcome not only to possibility but to one another. We kneel down on the ground together and let faith grow in the gaps of all we do not know. We become settled not because we are certain, but because we have learned to be people of *humility*, of *humus*, of the *earth*.

All We Do Not Know

One of my favorite stories in the Bible is from John 6. The day after feeding over five thousand people from a few loaves and some spare fish and then walking across the stormy sea, Jesus was met by a crowd—and they had questions (John 6:25-30):

"When did you get here?"

"What can we do to perform the works of God?"

"What sign, then, are you going to do so that we may see and believe you?"

Personally, I think their bellies were still thinking about the previous day's meal. They wanted more. But instead of replicating the miracle or giving direct answers to their questions, Jesus went on to give one of the more confusing teachings of his time: "I am the living bread that came down from heaven. If anyone eats of this bread he will live forever. The bread that I will give for the life of the world is my flesh" (John 6:51).

I imagine the people looked back at Jesus with deeply furrowed brows. Then they turned toward one another and in hushed tones asked, "How can this man give us his flesh to eat?" (v. 52).

Jesus continued, "Just as the living Father sent me and I live because of the Father, so the one who feeds on me will live because of me" (v. 57).

Well, the crowd had had enough at that point. It was as if Jesus were speaking another language. People started to leave. Even the disciples scratched their heads and grumbled among themselves, "This teaching is hard. Who can accept it?" (v. 60).

As the crowd began to disperse, Jesus turned to the remaining twelve and asked, "You don't want to go away too, do you?" (v. 67).

I wonder if it was silent for a moment, a pregnant pause filling the air as their eyes darted to one another and avoided direct line of sight with Jesus. Perhaps they glanced down at their feet, drawing circles with their toes in the Capernaum soil. But then Peter spoke first, "Lord, to whom will we go?" (v. 68).

I love that response. Peter did not deny he had questions. He did not try to play it off as if he didn't think Jesus' teaching sounded a little absurd. "Oh, yeah, sure . . . Eating flesh and blood? Got it. No problem." But as he watched people who had once walked with Jesus fade into the distance and looked back at the man he had come to know and love, Peter knew the answer would be found not through surety but through presence. He surveyed his options and knew that despite all the mystery that lingered around the person of Jesus, no answer could outweigh his nearness. His soul knew what his mind could not comprehend: "You are the Holy One of God" (v. 69). Compelled and curious, he stayed.

This story has become an anchor for all my unanswered questions, because while shared curiosity fosters humility, the humble path does not always lead us where we want to go. Good questions often multiply into more questions, which can leave us feeling a bit unmoored. A touch out of control. Mystery has that effect. But when we, like Peter, filter our not-knowing through a posture of humility and the person of Jesus, the urgency for answers decreases. We de-center ourselves from the story and turn our attention back to Jesus, and in that moment, we find a knowing that transcends the mind. We can close our eyes and almost imagine a gentle hand that has always rested on our shoulders, the breath of God running like a shiver down the spine. In the midst of our uncertainty, we discover what it looks like not only to be held but, in turn, to hold. Like Jesus, we can let the questions linger, because belonging is dependent not on neat and tidy answers but on presence in the midst of the questions.

By saying the questions out loud, we practice a shared curiosity. We hold out our uncertainties to one another as we pass the cup of Communion. We come face to face with our earthiness as our eternal longings hold hands with our limitations, because, like the psalmist, we recognize that "common people are only a vapor; important people, an illusion. Together on a scale, they weigh less than a vapor" (Psalm 62:9). No one is an expert, not really. While cherished, we are but dust in the hands of an almighty God. We are part of his beautiful whole, but still only a part—together less than a vapor when compared to his vastness. And the more we ask rather than answer, the more we see our wispiness amid the past, present, and future "cloud of witnesses" (Hebrews 12:1). We settle into our common finitude, held by One who is infinite. By practicing curiosity together, our sense of belonging expands and settles into the ground of humility, because as we put down our expertise, we learn to live within God's sacred mystery as if it were the warmth of stained-glass light.

Moving Closer

This practice is a hard one for me, because it's one thing to admit my questions to myself. It takes an entirely different kind of humility and courage to hold them out for others to see. But we also don't have to complicate it. To practice shared curiosity, consider taking your list of questions from the previous chapter and telling a trusted friend, spouse, therapist, priest, or pastor about the questions you are holding. If you simply want to say the questions out loud without additional hypothesizing, you may want to clarify that you are not asking for immediate answers but simply need another person to hold the questions alongside you. Perhaps give them space to voice their own questions. If you are both comfortable, you may even consider speaking the questions out loud to God. As you practice shared curiosity in your everyday life, I hope you will find reciprocity, a willingness to say and to hold questions together.

12

FROM BREADTH TO DEPTH

The risk is what allows for the possibility of the gift.

PRIYA PARKER

In 1992, my aunt and uncle sold their beach house, but every summer before that, family vacations were spent along the Lake Michigan shoreline. Growing up in predominantly landlocked Indiana, those July days were a dream. For an entire week, I would fill every possible moment with building sandcastles or burying my younger brother up to his neck. We'd run along the water's edge dodging waves, stopping only to collect shells that had washed ashore. Each day tasted like the fresh blueberries we bought from farm stands along the rural Michigan roads, and the air was filled with the scent of sunscreen and Fresca. I was perfectly content to sit along the lake's foamy edge, digging my sun-browned toes into the sand. Even now, I can close my eyes and feel the cool rush and retreat of the water beneath my body.

I loved Lake Michigan, and yet it frightened me. If you have never been to the Great Lakes, it's hard to anticipate the vastness of the waters. If it were not for the fresh water that lapped against the shore (and the blessed lack of jellyfish and sharks), you might be convinced you were standing on the edge of the ocean, because no matter how hard you strain your eyes, there's no seeing the other side of the lake. The waves behave like waves, and the tides creep in and back out. Seagulls stalk the beach for every forgotten potato chip or discarded hot dog. I really cannot undersell the greatness of the Great Lakes.

And I think it was that same immensity that scared me. No matter how warm and welcoming the waters, there was always a point where you could no longer see what prowled beneath your feet. It wasn't that I was a poor swimmer. I was part of a generation whose parents were instructed to toss their babies into pools hoping their instincts would kick in and their bodies would naturally learn to swim (mine did), so I have been in water before I could even walk. Swimming was not the issue. It was the depth that made me nervous. I knew the farther I waded in, the more mysteries lurked beneath the currents. The darker the waters became, the less I retained any sense of control. I could not yet spell my name but was already keenly aware of the risks of going deeper, so I kept my little body a safe distance to the shore.

The strange thing is that despite my uncertainty about the waters, I would have always chosen Lake Michigan over the Slip 'N Slide we had at home in our backyard or the community pool where Mom and Dad would take us on occasion, because despite how much those shallower waters provided the illusion of safety, possibility was alive amid the gradient deep.

The Shallows

I wish I could say I left my hesitation on the shores of Lake Michigan, but I did not. Despite how much I long for meaningful, authentic relationships, the depths can still elicit anxiety. That's one of the many wonky things about belonging—how we can want it and resist it at the same time. This tendency to fear what lies beyond the shallow end follows many of us into relationships. Most days, it seems easier to slide above the surface or shine a momentary spotlight on our best features rather than sit with another person in confession—to not only look upon the reality of our souls but for another set of eyes to bear witness. Like Adam and Eve in the Garden, shame sends us into hiding. We make a mad dash for the trees, grabbing leaves, bark, grass, or anything else to cover our nakedness. Before we have even given God or another person a chance, the threat sends us running.

We choose the shallows because life at the surface provides a perceived safety and minimal commitment. We can smile broadly on Sunday mornings, casting our hello-how-are-yous wide without offering more than a good-fine-busy in return. We can spread ourselves thin across social networks, being friendly with many but known by few, if at all. Please hear: these interactions are not inherently flawed. There is nothing wrong with giving others a small window into our lives, but when we want belonging, a square can only offer so much.

We are people of Communion, but instead of letting the goodness of a full-bodied wine dance upon our tongues, we often sip on overly sweetened Kool-Aid, a thin and cheap imitation of the sacred connection we crave. While dipping our toes into wide but shallow relational waters can sometimes scratch the itch of loneliness, other days, we walk away with hives. Our souls get even more snarled than when we started, even more aware of everything we are trying so hard to hide or carry on our own. The surface, while appearing safe, remains hollow.

I understand the fear. I really do. Every relationship comes with risk. Love opens us up to the possibility of being hurt, and when we have been wounded in the past, we are even more aware of pain's potential. Some of us carry deep scars that cannot be ignored. Many of our relational wounds are still open and raw, and the fear festers.

Over a decade into our marriage, I realized I had been holding parts of myself from my husband. It was complicated. Wounds from past relationships still stung, leaving me to wonder what others were hiding behind closed doors. Ben had given me no reason to distrust him, but about the time I laid my panic down, I'd hear yet another story of someone whose pastor or partner or friend had hidden huge chunks of their lives from the people closest to them. Combined with a nagging sense of not-enoughness, I was consistently pestered by two fears: *What if Ben is hiding something?* and *If I'm fully known, all the way down, will he stick around?* And the more my love for him increased, so did my fear.

I loved Ben more than any other person. (Still do.) Of all the human beings on the planet, from the first day we started dating, he has felt the most like home. But I could not shake the gnawing idea (that eventually turned into years of recurring bad dreams) that at some point Ben would turn out to be someone other than who I thought he was. Even after I walked down the aisle and years of faithful friendship left us laughing and carried us through the death of our son, opening myself up to Ben fully felt too great a risk. In the innermost part of my being, so hidden I often did not see it myself, I had one "just in case" bag packed and one hand on the door.

What often causes us to remain in the shallows is not the fear of being known but the fear of being abandoned. We wonder, *If I do this, that, or the other, will the other person stay?* We keep parts of ourselves close, even from our most intimate connections, because while we can choose isolation or try to control it, abandonment pulls the rug out from under us, leaving us lying on ground muddied by our own lack. Abandonment seethes, "You were right. You are not enough."

The pain and the fear of having a loved one leave are real. They are felt. They can shadow the waters of belonging far longer than we'd like. And I will not try to convince you that your tenderness and hesitancy are not legitimate.

But I have also learned that healing, wholeness, and connection are not found in the shallows. Aloneness is not the answer to the risks of intimacy, and spreading ourselves thin like peanut butter does not satisfy the soul but leaves us with a dry and wanting mouth. Breadth is not the solution to our desire for relational depth. Like Jesus holding out his hand to a shaking Peter, belonging calls us out into the water.

Redefining Safety

"What do you mean? I don't understand."

I looked at Ben beside me at the steering wheel, his eyes darting my direction as if searching my face for what to say next.

Uncertainty flickered behind his eyes as he tried to describe his recent spiritual wrestling, how he had been quietly questioning some previously held ideas and beliefs. Later, he would admit that in those moments he was afraid of how I might react. Perhaps he thought I would be mad or imagined some worst-case scenario that involved me asking him to turn the car around so I could gather up the kids and leave town without him. Nervousness can easily whip up some far-fetched tales. But to be honest, his hesitancy was justified. I have no poker face, so while my brain was trying to digest what he was telling me, I am sure my expression exuded nothing but a growing sense of fear. Early on, our shared beliefs had been one of the foundations of our marriage—something that aligned easily. Part of me assumed that synchronicity would always be there, that our spiritual paths would neatly coincide, so those first moments of hearing his questions felt like cracks forming in the concrete. My silence, I'm sure, was deafening.

What Ben did not realize is that everything inside me was panicking. Old anxieties about what people I loved might be hiding resurfaced and left me paralyzed. Part of me was frozen, while the other part wanted to run in the opposite direction. My mind and emotions were torn. But as I looked into Ben's eyes and listened to the man who had given me nothing but steady love, I knew that admitting his questions had cost him and left him relationally exposed. Something about the vulnerability Ben offered in the midst of such newfound waters began to gently dismantle the walls I built around my heart.

We didn't turn the car around that day. The more we talked, the more apparent it became that our spiritual paths were not so divergent as we once thought. Not neat and tidy mirror images, mind you, yet not cataclysmic contrasts either. And over the years, we have learned to be patient with the pieces of ourselves that are still becoming—to live and to love even amid the questions and differences. But that first conversation was a doozy that led us into the deepest waters of our married life. There was no sand beneath our feet. There were no life rafts or water wings to keep our heads above the waves. We could not see the other side. With nothing to hide behind or hold on to apart from each other, our fullest selves were on display. But the more we lingered in those untamed waters, floating in a new sea of the unknown, tenderness increased between us. A deeper love began to grow. And it was here we learned how to float.

When I think about those days and weeks after that car ride, I wonder how much I looked like Peter the day the storm raged and the disciples' boat was "battered by the waves, because the wind was against them" (Matthew 14:24). The man who sat beside me looked like my husband. He sounded like my husband. I was still drawn to him like my husband. And yet, like the disciples, I was terrified by the strength of the wind and wondered whether I too had seen a ghost.

But, just as Jesus responded to Peter that day as the weather threatened to overturn the boat, I sensed the same divine invitation not to run but to step further in: "Come" (Matthew 14:29). Like starfish, Ben and I stretched ourselves out upon the sea, holding on to each other with one hand and Jesus with the other as we rocked back and forth, up and down. I cannot explain what happened from there any more than to say a peace began to take hold inside me as I realized that even there, amid my deepest fears of abandonment and the unknown, I was held. And the farther we drifted out upon the water, God grabbed those bags I had packed within my heart, tossed them into the deep, and then turned toward me as if to say, "You won't be needing those."

Ben is my favorite human person, and figuring out life and God and family alongside him is one of my greatest joys. But even our closest relationships come with uncertainty. Safe is not the same as risk-free, because to love is to risk. Love that "bears all things, believes all things, hopes all things, endures all things" cannot linger on the shore (1 Corinthians 13:7). This all-ness has no shallow end, because love calls us out to dwell deeply with God and each other through moment-by-moment courage, curiosity, and surrender of control.

We are not safe because we are certain. We are safe because we are held. Just as the father went to find his lost sons and Jesus stretched his hand and "caught hold" of Peter, our God is a God of rescue. Because of the abundance of his love, we can stretch out our hands to one another. We can wade into the places where our feet cannot touch the floor, because God is already there, holding out his hand. The more we learn to follow him amid fears, the more we will find communion that is not dependent on the stillness of the waters. The more we will learn to dwell within the deep.

Beyond Ourselves

By now you know I have always been a little afraid of what love might require, and that panic has not been isolated to my marriage. For a long time, hearing about the lives of saints or missionaries or martyrs would produce a large, unwieldy knot in my stomach. Like a student avoiding the probing eyes of a teacher, I prayed I would not be called on, "Please, God. Not me." Admittedly, I am still a little that way, a little avoidant when I consider how often the pursuit of God holds hands with surrender. Love requires courage, but increasingly, I am less afraid. More and more, I can look at the life and words of faithful followers and instead of paralyzing fear find vestiges of hope.

In her 1979 Nobel Prize acceptance speech, Mother Teresa invited the crowd of people who had gathered in Norway to join her in the peace prayer of Saint Francis of Assisi. Their voices rose in unison:

> Lord, make me a channel of your peace,
> that where there is hatred, I may bring love;
> that where there is wrong, I may bring the spirit
>   of forgiveness;
> that where there is discord, I may bring harmony;
> that where there is error, I may bring truth;
> that where there is doubt, I may bring faith;
> that where there is despair, I may bring hope;
> that where there are shadows, I may bring light;
> that where there is sadness, I may bring joy.
> Lord, grant that I may seek rather to comfort than to
>   be comforted;
> to understand, than to be understood;
> to love, than to be loved.
> For it is by forgetting self, that one finds.
> It is by forgiving, that one is forgiven.
> It is by dying, that one awakens to eternal life.

What strikes me about this prayer and Mother Teresa's speech that followed is that her words were not romanticized admonitions of what love could be, but full of the names and faces of the people with whom Mother Teresa had lived—people who were widely forgotten, overlooked, destitute, and dying. When she said, "If we really believe, we will begin to love. And if we love, naturally, we will try to do something," she understood what it meant to dwell together in difficulty. She knew what she was asking of us. She was familiar with the cost. But this is what gets me: defying all earthly logic, Mother Teresa's experiences alongside the poor only seemed to cement the love of God inside her. By giving up the breadth of the world, her life only seemed to grow richer, fuller, more meaningful, so much so that she invited us to join her, "first in our own home, our next door neighbor, in the country we live, in the whole world." Love always moves us to go deeper.

To live beneath the surface alongside one another may not require us to pattern our lives in the exact footsteps of Mother Teresa or the apostle Paul or Martin Luther King Jr., but rather, like the saints who came before us, to let our common life be characterized by the love of Jesus, a love that begins right where we are but knows no bounds.

Belonging is not content to dig its toes into the sand; rather, it moves us from a posture of breadth to depth—with God and with each other. The two hold hands. Because as we step out of the shallows and into the waters, no matter how uncertain, we discover what it looks like to hold and to be held. It ushers us past our fears of abandonment and away from surface relationships to a place that—against all odds—feels an awful lot like Home. Because it is here that love evolves from a good idea to a way of being, as belonging compels us out beyond ourselves.

Looking Inward

To trade a posture of breadth for depth, we must consider the barriers that consistently keep us in the shallows. We must ask, *Where is fear lurking?* You can begin by reflecting on past or current relationships, because they are often a good window to see your personal patterns of anxieties and internal resistance. With the names and faces of specific people in mind, you can ask yourself these questions: *What makes me afraid to go deeper? What am I holding back from my closest relationships? What am I trying to protect?*

13

CIRCLES OF BELONGING

By laying bare and facing the worst of ourselves,
we reveal the very best of ourselves.

LEONARD SWEET

I walked out of the house and into the darkness toward the car as a familiar dread passed through me: *I had shared too much.* Remorse settled on my shoulders as my friend Kathleen climbed into the driver's seat next to me. She started the engine, but we sat quietly in the car a few moments before shifting into drive. I could feel her glance at me as I sat quietly, replaying the evening's conversation in my mind.

Kathleen and I had been reading through a book along with two other friends, meeting every few weeks to drink coffee and discuss a few chapters. I loved our evenings together, but as the weeks progressed, it felt strange to be with them while keeping parts of my story close, concealed like shadows behind a curtain. I have always been protective of my marriage, always wanting to retain a sacredness between me and Ben even when we are angry or do not agree. But we were in those early days of his spiritual wrestling, and while the intimate details were ours, I knew I needed more hands to hold. I was tired of the ruminating thoughts turning cartwheels in my mind and carrying the weightiness of my emotions. I was weary of showing up but keeping slivers of myself hidden. You can only smile so long before your face begins to hurt. That night, I did not know exactly how my friends might respond to the journey Ben and I were on, but I knew I needed to say words out loud.

We sat around in sweatpants, sipping decaf, and I began to talk, my chest tightening with a strange mix of nervousness and hope. All eyes were on me. Heads nodded. Eyebrows furrowed slightly. In the moment, I could not tell whether their stoic expressions were the result of intent listening or disapproval, but words kept spilling out of me anyway. *You opened this door, so you might as well keep walking through it . . .* At some point, someone handed me a tissue.

Silence followed. I don't know whether the pause in conversation was really that long or became exaggerated in my mind due to the sheer amount of nerves pulsing through me. All I know is that in the minutes after I was done talking until the time I walked out the door that evening, regret began to fester inside me. Slippery voices tickled the back of my brain: *you have done it again. You have said too much.*

In the early years after our son's death, knowing when or how or why to share the raw parts of my story always seemed tricky, and I often got it wrong. The more I stepped toward others in friendship, the more I craved the freedom of being my full self. I wanted to be known. But in my hastiness, I often cannonballed into the deep end before even dipping a toe into the waters. The result usually left me huffing and puffing with remorse as I tried to swim back to the edge, looking at all the now-drenched people who had been unprepared to be splashed.

What I did not realize in those early days was that, very much like Lake Michigan or the pool where I take our boys in the summer, the deep did not happen all at once. Rather, there was a gradient descent. Toes came before ankles, ankles before shins, shins before knees—you get the picture. Going deep often requires a period of easing in. Our minds, bodies, and emotions need time to adjust to the waters, to convince ourselves, "Okay. That's not so bad. Maybe just a little bit more."

So much of creation is patterned this way. Slow. Gradual. Pregnant bellies become babies that turn into toddlers until day by day skin stretches and bones grow into full-fledged adults. Winter lasts forever, ice glazing sidewalks and rooftops, until one day a thaw settles beneath the earth and greens the ground. Spring arrives, followed by summer and then autumn and, then again, winter. Even the sun does not arrive like the flip of a switch, but gently as day and night fade into one another.

Modern life often resists the gradualness of things, preferring instant gratification instead. We microwave our hot dogs, stream TV shows so we do not have to bother with commercials, and order books to be delivered on our doorstep the next day. Immediacy has become the expectation, not only in what we consume but in the ways we become and belong. We expect friendships to flourish with the click of a button, and while we might be more social than ever, we are often far from connected. Because more often than not, depth is gradual. Intimacy is not instant but practiced through steady and faithful movements toward one another over time.

Campfires and Confessions

Back when I worked in college residential life, one of the first things we did with student leaders to prepare them for the year ahead was pile them into twelve-passenger vans and take them into the woods for a retreat. They'd bond over shared experiences of mess hall dining or mosquitoes pestering them in the dead of night. They'd double over in laughter upon realizing they'd forgotten to bring underwear or recalling the paddles lost kayaking earlier that day. But the entire weekend seemed to hinge on stories that emerged around campfires. As flames danced in the inner circle, one by one students offered a little window into their souls. Past wounds seemed easier to speak into the night, where they could not fully see each other's faces. Many went to bed feeling a little bit exposed, but the next morning, as students lumbered into breakfast and others scooted over to make room for them at the table, a communal sigh of relief gave rise to a new spirit of connection.

I understood their angst. Vulnerability is a key ingredient to knowing and being known, but sharing ourselves with others comes with risk. Rarely do we want to be the one who goes first, the one who holds themselves out upon the waters and hopes no one will splash them in the face. Not everyone receives our revelations with kindness, and yet, we cannot experience belonging without being willing to step out of the boat.

As Curt Thompson writes, "We need others to bear witness to our deepest longings, our greatest joys, our most painful shame, and all the rest in order to have any sense at all of ourselves." We cannot know our truest selves apart from one another, and confession ties our humanity together, shining a light upon all the ways our souls overlap.

Through the regular practice of confession, we lay ourselves out upon the table. We open up as an offering, because while risky, vulnerability is how we step toward the call to "love your neighbor as yourself" (Matthew 22:39). It is where we live out the uncanny way of the kingdom, where "power is made perfect in weakness" and shared humanity becomes our common ground (2 Corinthians 12:9 ESV). It is where your story becomes absorbed into the larger story as you say the words out loud.

Vulnerability begins with us. It begins with a willingness to show up as the truest, unvarnished versions of ourselves, no matter the outcomes. It is speaking our stories into the night across fire pits, unsure whether anyone will stick around until morning. Confession of all kinds requires courage, because revelation is a risk. Perhaps this is why Jesus so often told his disciples to "shake the dust," knowing that not all places and people would return the welcome (Matthew 10:14; Mark 6:11; Luke 9:5). But here's the good news for you and me: our confessions do not need to come all at once.

Revelation

As a mom of four boys, there has been a good deal more nakedness in our home than I anticipated, especially during their younger years. For a period, I had to ban the animated *Tarzan* from our movie rotation, because without fail, fifteen minutes into the jungle story, I would walk into the family room to find wild boys in underwear, jumping from coffee table to couch. And it didn't matter who was there. Grandma. A neighbor. The UPS man. The moment *Tarzan* came on, the clothes came off.

While I have come to accept a certain measure of shirtlessness, I have also had to insert some lessons about modesty—about how much we reveal based on the people we are around. Running around in boxer briefs is fine when you're playing in the basement with a brother. Go crazy. But sunning yourself buck naked on the driveway while our neighbor lady Brenda walks by with her dog? Not okay.

Because here's the thing: how much we reveal matters—in our homes, yes, but also in our relationships.

When it comes to practicing vulnerability, I have had to learn there is a distinct difference between authenticity and transparency. In a culture where we treat online spaces like personal confessionals or hide behind shiny smiles, we often confuse the two. We tend to say too much or too little. Our vulnerability leans toward the extremes, either leaving ourselves wide open to the masses or shutting ourselves off from even those who are safe.

But "true belonging," as Brené Brown writes, "doesn't require you to change who you are; it requires you to be who you are." Authenticity is showing up as your true self—your personality and preferences, your likes and dislikes, your fashion and passions. You're a loud snorter at the movies? Great. Welcome. You're a fan of socks with Crocs? Cool. Come on in. You're passionate about conservative politics or climate change or monster trucks? Awesome. Bring that too. To be authentic, all you have to be is you.

But here is the kicker: while authenticity is about being real, transparency is about *how much* you reveal. You can be yourself without exposing everything to all people all at once. Not every moment of every day is a confessional. Rather, like the gradient part of the pool, you can ease your way into relationships, because while authenticity is for all, transparency takes trust and reciprocity developed over time. You can be genuine but go gently, with yourself and others.

Too-much transparency or too-soon transparency only leaves us naked on the driveway, sunburnt in tender places and wishing for a towel, while our poor neighbors don't know whether to laugh, look away, or keep walking. Such unbridled nakedness is not kind to anyone, really. (Sorry, Brenda. Truly.)

Sacred Space

I have heard the phrase "your body is a temple" used by fitness gurus to peddle their latest products, their uncomfortably large, bulging arms waving and pointing wildly at me on the other side of the screen. I look at my own arms and then down at my belly, how silver streaks have formed in the wake of pregnancies and age. Momentary guilt flickers and then fades. Yes, perhaps I should take more spin classes, eat fewer french fries, and care for the delicate contours of my skin. But I do not think that's what the apostle Paul had in mind. When Paul urged the people of God to treat their bodies as temples, his words were not a guilt-ridden ploy to promote fitness, one more trek to Jerusalem or hike along the Corinthian shore, but rather, a reminder that like the Judaic tabernacle, each person houses a sacredness within their skin.

Since the days the Israelites wandered in the desert, the tabernacle was considered the *Mishkan*, the dwelling place of God. Everywhere the people moved, God moved with them by tent through the wilderness and then eventually within the elaborate walls built by King Solomon. The temple was divided into three parts that grew increasingly smaller and more sacred. Only the high priest could enter the innermost room due to the reverence and ritual required for what was considered the most holy place.

So when Paul, a learned man who was quite familiar with the concept and history of the tabernacle, compared the fleshy bodies of the Corinthian people to this revered space, he understood the full ramifications of his words. When he said, "Don't you know that your body is a temple of the Holy Spirit who is in you, whom you have from God?" he knew he was telling believers that they, like the temple, had become a dwelling, a Mishkan, for the manifest presence of God. They held a holiness that should not be entered lightly.

You, too, are a temple. Contained within all the layers of your humanity, at the innermost center of your being, dwells the Holy Spirit of God himself. The Divine lingers with holy hush in your "inward parts," where God alone knew you since the days you were hidden in the depths of your mother (Psalm 139:13). These unseen nooks and crannies are where you can abide in freedom with the Father, a place where you exchange secrets in a language completely your own. A language that does not change with place and people but is the eternal language of Home.

Here, in this most sacred inner circle, you can speak freely, knowing that everything is already seen, already known, already inhabited. Everything is laid bare as transparency and transcendence swirl together like smoke and incense. You do not have to censor or hide or shine your confession but can bring them like a priest into the temple: broken, bloodied, held in a posture of surrender.

Belonging begins here, because depth matures not only gradually but in circles. A great sigh of relief comes with the realization you do not have to let everyone enter the tender corners of your soul. Rather, your most intimate confessions can begin with God and then turn outward, expanding in concentric circles of belonging. Ring by ring, the circles grow wider. Each one is a little more populated but a little less exposed. People may move in and out in seasons, as life ebbs and flows, but the center never shifts, freeing you to be authentic with all but exposed to only a few.

You do not have to go deep with everyone, because embracing a posture of welcome does not mean being the answer to everyone's loneliness. By doing so, we drown. We gasp and sputter beneath waves of scarcity that crash and call, "If not you, then who?" And while the storm might appeal to the ego, the cheap thrill of being wanted, nothing can save you outside the holy hush that remains in the sacred center of your soul. As Parker Palmer writes, "Yes, we are created in and for community, to be there, in love, for one another. But community cuts both ways: when we reach the limits of our own capacity to love, community means trusting that someone else will be available to the person in need."

To say "you are welcome" means that you are a finite temple who is invited to live and love in the fullness of the One who dwells within you. You are invited to create circles of belonging and practice discernment about who will inhabit the inner places. But to say "you are welcome" is also to believe that the same abundance found within you is held within the folds of the other person. You can offer yourself in love, kindness, warmth, and compassion, without being the one who holds every hand along the way.

The Ones Who Stay

That night, as I sat in the darkness of Kathleen's car, I wondered what my friends were thinking. In silence, our brains seem to instinctively fill in our gaps of knowing with stories. These stories may be generous, hopeful even, but if you're like me, the internal narrative tends to spiral and spin out quickly. Old defaults of fear and abandonment stand ready to catch me, ready to sink their claws into my psyche.

But I did not have to wonder long or go through the two-day process of retreat, renewal, and then return into relationship (a pattern ingrained inside me like a well-worn path). No, as Kathleen put the car in drive and pulled out onto the gravel country road, her gentle voice broke the silence. "I just want you to know I'm glad you shared tonight. I know you might be feeling a little remorse right now, but I hope you know I'm glad you told us those things."

Everything that had begun to twist inside me loosened. I did not realize I had been holding my breath until I took a deep drag of summer air, letting its warm freshness swirl around inside me. Relief spread like cool water down a dry and weary throat.

I exhaled as tears gathered one more time in the corners of my eyes, "Thank you. That means a lot."

And it did. That night seemed to solidify a steadiness between me and that small circle of friends. I knew I could confess my secrets and they would stay. I knew I could shine a light behind my dusty, musty curtains and they would not distance themselves from the less-polished pieces of my humanity but move closer, handing me love, acceptance, the occasional tissue, and a little more of themselves.

Moving Closer

One way to practice transparency is to determine who is in your circles of belonging and how you can gradually move closer in this season. On a piece of paper or in a journal, draw five concentric circles, each one getting a little bigger than the one before it. (Kind of like a Russian Matryoshka doll.) At the sacred center, write "Jesus" or "God" or whatever name of God you choose, to remember that he is at our core. In the next two layers of circles, write down the names of the people you consider your closest relationships. The actual number of people in these smaller circles is not important (I have two or three in the smallest circle and somewhere between six to eight in the next). But remember: the smaller the circle, the greater trust and transparency you have with those individuals. The two outer circles are for casual friends and acquaintances.

Once you've created your circles, picture the people in your smallest circle and prayerfully consider these questions:

In this season, how can I go deeper with this group of people?

Are there ways I can be more transparent or invite vulnerability?

Do I need to reallocate relational energy from the wider circles to invest in the people closest to me?

You may decide to ask the same question of the larger circles, if you want, but as you think or write through these questions, jot down some ideas of how you'd like to move closer in the coming months.

Please note: I like to revisit these circles seasonally, because relationships bend and flex with time (as does our relational capacity). If you are currently in a season of feeling disconnected or are struggling to come up with names to put in your inner circles, perhaps you can think of two or three people who you would like to move toward more intentionally in this season. Ask God to help you maintain an open hand and remember that relationships grow slowly, not every connection will deepen, and being a person of welcome often requires a measure of waiting and perseverance.

14

FROM CONSUME TO CREATE

| By means of your light we see light. |

PSALM 36:9

During our first year of marriage, Ben and I had six friends: Ross, Rachel, Monica, Chandler, Phoebe, and Joey. Every night, we would pop in the latest *Friends* DVD that arrived from Netflix (back when Netflix mailed you physical copies of shows and movies and you had to wait a week to find out what happened next). We laughed. We cried. We didn't get off our secondhand couch.

Watching six twentysomethings navigate young adulthood together gave us the sense that we were not alone, so for that, I am grateful. But the cast of *Friends* became like surrogates, stand-ins for the community we really wanted. There was something about sitting by ourselves watching other people's pretend lives that was so much easier than going out of our apartment to make real friends of our own. We chalked it up to being newlyweds at the time (and there was some truth in that), but the unspoken reality neither of us was ready or desperate enough to face is that we craved belonging. We wanted connection outside the two of us, but instead of getting off the couch, we consumed a cheapened version of friendship that had a ten-season expiration date from the beginning.

The Myth of More

The problem with putting the pressure of belonging on a specific place or person is that we begin to see each other for what we can gain. We network with other professionals, hoping to walk away with new clients or connections to get ahead. We say yes to getting coffee, not out of genuine care or desire but to maintain the persona of someone who cares. We date, not because we really like who the other person is but because we like who we are when we are around them. Without even realizing it, consumerism leaks into our relationships. The person becomes a means to an end.

How can it not? Particularly within the United States, consumerism is core to so many of our cultural values of success and greatness. To be more, we must have more. More money. More assets. More knowledge. More influence. *More* promises a life of ease and contentment, but that accumulation comes with a cost. More output requires more input—more time, more energy, more stress, more fatigue upon the body, and more relationships placed upon the fringes. And what do we find when we arrive, when we attain the thing or the status for which we've been reaching? A momentary buzz, perhaps. A little time in the spotlight. But sooner or later, that "more" fades to black. The high of success subsides, and we are left wondering, *Now what?*

I recently read a few celebrity memoirs, and while the individual details are different, the storylines are largely the same.

The narrative goes a little something like this: a sense of lack followed me as I grew up, so I threw myself into a life of performance trying to fill in those gaps with fame, money, sex, drugs, ridiculously huge houses, and an entourage who wanted to be close to it all. I got everything I wanted, but it was not enough. In the eyes of all my peers, I had made it, but the gaping hole was still there. It was only then—when I had everything—that I realized life is not about what you can get but what you can give. Only then do we begin to find contentment.

Their stories remind me of the book of Ecclesiastes. King Solomon had it all. Wealth. Wives. Power. Pleasure. Authority. Food. Drink. Even wisdom. But as he looked out on his kingdom and all that he had acquired, he assessed his gain with five gut-punching words: "Absolute futility. Everything is futile" (Ecclesiastes 1:2).

What a downer, right? It's enough for us to throw our hands in the air and scream, *So then what in the world is the point?* Good question. In fact, I am pretty sure that was the very question Solomon and so many celebrities since him have asked at one time or another. If more is not the answer, then what is?

Here is the sneaky thing about approaching the world as consumers: more never fulfills its promises. The shell might be shiny, but the inside is empty because consumerism is built around scarcity. All we see is what we do not have, so our posture becomes one of grasping. We view everything through the lens of what we can gain (bigger, better, faster). Even people become commodities, and relationships become a way to get what we want.

Most of the time, it's not intentional. Consumerism is so embedded in the fabric of our culture that we do not see the ways we are all unraveling beneath its weight. But it's there, silently pushing us all toward empty visions of greatness and away from the true belonging for which we were created.

The Way of Less

Nearly twenty years after binge-watching *Friends*, I picked up Matthew Perry's memoir (because of course I did). To this day, I carry a measure of gratitude for our pseudo-friends, particularly the guy named Chandler whose physical comedy and inflection still find its way into my daily discourse. "Could I *BE* any hungrier?"

I was prepared to be disappointed. Rarely do people we know from a distance step perfectly into their personas when we encounter them a little closer. But as I listened to his story, I found his complexity refreshing. His openness about his struggles with drug and alcohol addiction as well as his fumblings through fame and relationships did not mar the image of Chandler from *Friends* but rather made him more accessible. More human. Another person just trying to find his way Home.

That's the point at which I leaned in a little closer. It was not Perry's rise to more that compelled me. It was the way, through his words, he invited me into a lesser version of himself. I do not know all his motivations in writing the book. But what I do know is that at some point, Perry made the choice to tell a truer story, one not perpetuated by *People* magazine or paparazzi but one that is raw, gritty, and (I hope) a little more real.

He postured himself as a creator, offering all that he had in love to the world.

Is that not the way of the Divine? God's first relationship with the world and humanity was as its Creator. Out of utter nothingness, he spoke, and goodness moved from his mouth into mountains, rivers, glowing orbs, and vibrant greens. Out of dust, he formed the first person, whose body and soul became a house for his essence. But he did not stop there. From front to back, the Bible narrative reveals how God continues to enter helpless, hopeless situations and create all things new, around us and in us and with us. He is a God who entered the world not as an overlord but as an infant, making himself less in the gaze of the world knowing it was the only way to give us more.

Then God went and did something even more ridiculous. Not only did he establish himself as Creator of the world and of everything good that is in it, but he invited us to join him. God created us to be creators. As world-famous painter Makoto Fujimura writes, "We are *Imago Dei* . . . , and we are by nature creative makers." All of us. Creativity is not reserved for the elite, for a certified group of painters, poets, sculptors, musicians, authors, or artists. To be creative is to be human. By forming us in his image, he welcomes us to join him in his ongoing work of beauty flowering out of cracks and crevices. He invites us to bend a knee and watch abundance unfold in a kingdom where "the last will be first, and the first last" (Matthew 20:16). He gives us eyes to see our common, often-unnoticed lives as containers of his goodness, where from mustard seeds sprout beauty and life.

In all the ways consumerism demands more and then robs us blind, the way of a creator leans toward less. It's not rational. It's not pragmatic. It's terrifying to most of us who have grown up with Westernized ideals of comfort and ease, because being a creator demands that we begin with nothing. But the way of a creator is full of hope, not in what we can gain but what we can give, because when we see the world as a creator, we no longer see an empty pothole but an earthen vessel ready to be filled. The narrative is no longer a story of scarcity but one of abundance, because unlike consumers, a creator knows that out of nothing comes everything.

Being a creator frees us to belong to each other, because we can begin to move closer not for what we can gain but for what we can give. We can go into the grocery store and instead of seeing a grouchy old man behind the counter, see a person equally loved by God. We can tell a more generous story not only about ourselves but about each other, because we know that in the end, we are all just flesh and bones, we are all looking across the landscape of the earth and wondering where we fit. As creators, we can stand on equal footing, because dust becomes our common ground.

We can embrace the way of less, trusting as Parker Palmer writes that "by allowing something to die when its time is due, we create conditions under which new life can emerge." Our finitude becomes our freedom, a place where beauty can emerge and where we can (in the midst of all that is futile) "fear God and keep his commands" to love the Lord deeply and extend that embrace to one another (Ecclesiastes 12:13).

A Generative Life

Author Ben Palpant, in his book *Letters from the Mountain*, was the first to introduce me to the idea of generativity. Palpant writes primarily to writers (people dedicated to a craft), but the premise of generativity extends beyond the artist. It is a framework not only for those of us who put words on a page or apply brushstrokes to a canvas but whose creativity is manifested in making spreadsheets, diagnosing patients, packing boxes, and planning meals. Generativity is for all of us, because the concept is rooted in the idea that we are all creators, and unlike consumers, creators do their good work as a faithful act of love. Generativity gives with an open hand and inspires us to do the same.

I love the way Ben Palpant describes what generative people look like. He writes:

> I glance around the pews and see my friends—beloved children of God—emanating hope, redemption, insight, and transcendence. They pray when I'm unable, listen when I'm distracted, sing in my stead. They inspire a God-hunger in me, compelling me to do something meaningful with my life.

The work of a creator is not glamorous. The posture is not "look at me" but "here, this is for you." It is an intentional emptying of ourselves, a willingness to be vulnerable in everything we do so that even in the most mundane aspects of our lives we discover what it means to love "God with all your heart, with all your soul, and with all your mind" and to "love your neighbor as yourself" (Matthew 22:37-39). Generativity happens in the daily details of our lives, as we let our God-hunger infiltrate all that we do and how we see the world. Generativity moves us toward each other, away from outcomes and toward offerings. We move from living with a closed fist to loving with an open hand.

My friend Emily has an incredible way of living a generative life. A young mom in her early thirties, Emily chose to pause her professional career to be home with her two young kids. Since my boys are all in school these days, I pop by Emily's house on occasion for a cup of coffee and an hour of conversation. The moment I enter the door, I am greeted with warmth. She pours me a cup of black coffee, and we sit down at her dining room table as her kids come and go. None of these acts are particularly extraordinary, but it is Emily's caring presence and thoughtful questions that invite me to settle in. Emily is a brilliant question asker. I can tell she has spent time thinking about what she might want to ask before I get there, and as a result, our chats are always rich and deeply meaningful. I walk away feeling alive with curiosity and connectedness. Our conversations have fueled so much of the exploration of this book as well as how we live out our belonging within our church and our city.

Emily's ability to tap into her own wonderings and welcome people into those questions is generativity in action, because she does not hoard her curiosity but invites others in. Her vulnerability unlocks transparency in other people. I feel safe and seen in her presence, because she enters into a conversation ready to give, and that is a creative gift.

We often think about creativity in terms of perfection and performance or what we can gain in the making. But true creativity is birthed out of love. It is the ability to turn the ordinary corners of our lives into extraordinary beauty. Whether we are having a conversation or folding the laundry or asking our grocer about his day, these little moments become avenues for love to become manifest in and through us. I once heard Helena Sorensen say that making is "the journey of loving things into being" and that idea stuck with me. The Creator God did not breathe life into our lungs to leave it there, but so that through our exhale, his love might inhabit the world.

Do not get me wrong: the creative life is not a sexy life. It is not filled with mountain views and butterflies and sunsets. Creativity often requires us to dig up parts of ourselves we would rather remain unseen. It dares us to hope even when the darkness is as thick as tar and asks us to live openly, which often leaves us exposed. As a writer, sharing my words can feel like I'm standing shirtless in the middle of Target, the saggy skin and stretch marks that run like tiny rivers across my belly on display for all to see. "Gosh, that's a whole lot of skin," I sigh, fully aware of my imperfections. But most days, these fleshy words are all I have, so I offer them. I hold my breath for a moment and then exhale, having no idea where the words will land or how they will be held.

But the beauty of taking a creative posture in the world is that no matter how our offerings are received, the act in and of itself is good. What we give is no longer dependent on the whims of the market or on multiplying our investment, because as generative people, we do not give with the expectation of return but with the love of release. We become people marked not by fame but by faithfulness. Rooted in the abundance of a Creator God, our imaginations become free to create beauty out of all the seemingly insignificant specks of dust.

Perhaps Madeleine L'Engle said it best (as Madeleine L'Engle tends to do):

> Artists have always been drawn to the wild, wide elements they cannot control or understand—the sea, the mountains, fire. To be an artist means to approach the light, and that means to let go our control, to allow our whole selves to be placed with absolute faith in that which is greater than we are.

As people of welcome, we move from consumers to creators. We open wide our hands, and in doing so, become bearers of a light "greater than we are" right where we are.

Looking Inward

Moving from a consumer to a creator posture may feel clunky at first, but we can begin by paying attention to where consumerism might be lurking. We can ask ourselves: *Where am I more inclined to grasp than to give?* A good tell for me is when envy causes me to clench my teeth or I feel buried beneath a sense of lack. Maybe, for you, scarcity pops up in the form of fear or the instinct to hide or pull away. Being openhanded isn't easy and does require familiarity with the ways we can keep a tight fist.

On the flip side, we don't have to wait until we rid ourselves of consumerism before we walk the path of a creator. My pastor friend Steve DeNeff once noted how often we waste so much energy trying to eliminate vices that we never get around to cultivating the virtue. So while recognizing where consumerism might be living within us is good, we can also consider how we can live generatively. We can ask ourselves (and maybe even create a list): *How can I offer beauty, light, and love in this season? In what ways can I practice openhandedness with who I am and what I have?*

15

SEEDS OF CONFETTI

> It is hard work to live into this generative love,
> and it is what we are made for: to paint light
> into darkness, to sing in co-creation,
> to take flight in abundance.

MAKOTO FUJIMURA

I often think about that six-year-old version of me. Eyes bright. Hands free. Picnic tables full of neighborhood friends I had gathered for cake and ice cream. The image appears in my mind like a Polaroid, and that old, familiar longing rises up within me. While so much of life is becoming, figuring out who we are and how we relate, I wonder whether most of us are just trying to make our way back to some original versions of ourselves—back to when we did not hesitate to let sticky Popsicles run down our faces or to celebrate wild and free.

From the beginning, we humans have had a way of missing the beauty in front of us by zeroing in on the one thing we do not have but think we need. Envy is an itch we all scratch from time to time. But is it more than that? Are comparison and discontent strapped to our DNA, pulsing through our veins like an inherited disease since that day in the Garden? Does shame follow us like a shadow? I do not blame Eve or Adam. If it were not them, perhaps it would have been me who snatched the fruit.

Like the elder son in Jesus' story of the father and his lost boys, how often we miss the love that is already with us because our eyes were fixed elsewhere. Clouded by envy, we end up grasping for things not intended for our good and lose sight of the celebration that is unfolding. Despite the invitation of the Father, we sulk. Envy escalates into anger. We refuse to go inside. In a moment ripe with restoration—a brother or sister coming home—we struggle to see beyond what we lack because comparison blinds us to the beauty.

Jesus' story does not have a neat and tidy ending, leaving us to wonder whether the elder son ever went inside. Did he see the look of love in his father's eyes or stop trying to work the land to earn favor? Did he trade performance for presence, learning to see himself and his father beyond what he could gain? Did the older son ever go home and say hello to his brother? We don't know.

But how might the story have been different if he had? How might the narrative have shifted if instead of looking at his brother's return as a threat, he let himself witness the splendor of that moment and embraced his brother? What if, instead of pacing in the dirt, he went inside, grabbed a party popper, and participated in the celebration? What might have happened next?

Practicing Celebration

The moment we begin to side-eye one another, taking account of what you have that I don't, we diminish the love of God in and among us. Consumerism fuels comparison, and comparison kills community. We fall back into our grasping ways, treating ourselves and each other as commodities, counting up skills and talents, weighing one human against the other. As envy grows, we close our fists around what we think is ours— our piece of the pie, our slice of the cake, our seat at the table. Instead of moving toward one another with generosity and love, we pull back in self-protection. We seethe until comparison morphs into bitterness that darkens into hate. As James wrote, "For where there is envy and selfish ambition, there is disorder and every evil practice" (James 3:16). Envy is a slippery slope. The more we consume, the more we become consumed.

The optimist in me wants to believe that in the story of the lost sons the older brother had a reckoning. I want to imagine that his bitterness fell away in the eyes of his father and he ran inside to wrap forgiving arms around his brother. But I also recognize the chasm comparison often forms, a gap that is not easy to bridge if we do not remember "everything is yours" and shift our posture from one who consumes to one who creates.

Perhaps the father knew what he was doing by throwing a party. By barbecuing the best goat and putting aside work in the middle of the day, maybe intuition told him that there is no antidote to envy more potent than the practice of celebration.

In all the ways envy caves inward, celebration turns us toward one another. While envy is rooted in scarcity, celebration expands in abundance. Envy tells us to cling to what is ours, but celebration opens our palms. Envy causes us to pull back, to protect our turf, but celebration opens the door, pulls out a chair, and says, "Come over here! Have a seat by me." The practice of celebration invites us to see the good in ourselves and each other without intimidation or threat, remembering that the essence of God is in us both.

Please know we are not talking about the sparkly kind of celebration that applies silver linings to raging clouds or brushes away the darkness with sing-song admonitions of "everything happens for a reason!" No, shininess is not celebration but avoidance, a cheapening of the hard and holy work of seeing God's reflection in people and places. True celebration is bearing witness to a world that is not yet finished and naming the good we see along the way. True celebration groans toward the glory that emanates from a Creator God. Celebration is aware of the shadows but alive with hope. And when we celebrate, we set aside our white-knuckled ways in order to pay attention and participate in the slow, resilient beauty of redemption. We learn what it is to delight not only in God but in each other, to look out at faces and places and say, "It is good. Very good."

People and Places

Six years ago, we moved into our current house. It's the longest since Ben and I have been married that we have lived in one place. Life and career and an affinity toward flipping houses has kept us mobile. When our fifth son arrived on the scene, we were stretched thin and craved the proximity of grandparents. But moving back to our home state of Indiana was not easy.

Perhaps there is a perfect Venn diagram where people, culture, location, and season of life overlap to create these magical moments of belonging. Maybe sometimes we just get lucky. All I know is that some places we call home because they are known and familiar, but some places are home because they know us. For me and Ben, that place was Murfreesboro, Tennessee. Living there felt as if we were found. Everything just fit, which made leaving so very difficult.

Coming back to Indiana, I was reluctant to be around people who had experienced former versions of me and a little ashamed of how I inwardly rolled my eyes every time someone complained about how it took fifteen minutes to get across town. I longed for the safety of my best friend Cynthia in Tennessee, who knew the version of me with unbrushed teeth and hair that hadn't been washed in three days. The me who loved motherhood but always felt as if other parts of myself were put on hold every time the pregnancy test turned positive. The me in process. Cynthia's persistent friendship had taught me so much of what it means to live and love well, to be the one who goes first, and I mourned that our seven-minute separation had become seven hours.

Unlike our time in Tennessee, community back in Indiana did not come quickly. My love of place grew even slower still. While I wanted to look back over my shoulder in comparison, I sensed a growing invitation into a new way of belonging.

About that time I read Dietrich Bonhoeffer's book *Life Together*. While published in the 1950s, his words became a hand to hold in that season of transition. They are words I need to hold still. He writes, "He who loves his dream of a community more than the Christian community itself becomes a destroyer of the latter, even though his personal intentions may be ever so honest and earnest and sacrificial." I highlighted the words in neon yellow, and in the book's margins, I drew a large star, because I knew they were words I would have to return to as I learned to let go of my romanticized ideals and embrace the very real life that was unfolding in front of me.

Living here on the fringes of a rural city is not glamorous. Many days I step out onto the porch to be greeted by the smell of nearby farms, the musk of manure lingering in my nose long after I've gone back inside. But little by little, this place and its people are working their way into my being. I am learning to not only recognize but also celebrate the goodness that streams through my kitchen window, painting warm light across the chipped linoleum. I have started anticipating the ever-changing sky that opens up like a canvas above the farmlands on our drive to school.

But that growing affection has not been confined to place. A year or two after moving, I invited a few women to gather with me for what we have come to call Supper Club. Once a month, we eat together, catch up, and take turns bringing two questions to the table. Like tea that needs time to steep, our relationships have grown slow and steady. But life accumulates over time, and over the last three years, Ashleigh, Toni, Bailey, Kathleen, and I have walked through deaths and disappointments, jobs ending and jobs beginning, kids going off to school and kids moving back home, plus a slew of celebrations (that usually involve a dessert from Toni). We have brought it all to the table. And while we may not see each other much outside this small gathering, faithfully showing up for one another month after month has added up, turning a group of women into some of my dearest friends.

The more I savor this place and these people, the more love grows within me. The more I look for beauty across the flat lands, the more I see myself in the dark, rich soil. The more I water seeds of connection, the more I find sustenance at the table and the urge to throw my arms high above my head. The more I embrace celebration as a way of being, the more appreciation becomes gratitude and blossoms into contentment. The more I seek to know, the more I am known.

A life of welcome is not dependent on particular places or people, but belonging is not completely detached from them either. Because when we begin to look for and call out the good we see right where we are, celebration becomes a liturgy that leans toward hope. Sometimes hope is small. Very, very small. It is one blue sky after forty-five days of gray or the gentleness of a stranger who helps pick up spilled groceries off the pavement. But the more we can turn outward, expectant that God is creating and recreating in our midst, the more people and places become vessels of welcome. We can look for goodness right where we are and gather others together in expectation.

When we practice celebration, we scatter seeds of welcome like confetti. Some might fall upon the dusty soil. Some might bounce off the worn and weathered concrete. Not all will return the welcome. But others will sink down deep into the earth and take root. Belonging will grow in unlikely places alongside people we would not have expected, because the welcome of God is ripe with possibility. Love often defies the odds, and celebration urges us to keep an open hand, helping us know when to plant and when to let go.

When Belonging Fades

I talked with my mom not long ago about belonging. Mom has always been more social than I am, faster to reach out and invite in and say hello. She has always been eager to take zucchini bread or a pot of vegetable soup to the neighbors. But even now in her mid-sixties, Mom confided how in many ways, she feels more disconnected than ever. Once again, she finds herself in a season of wondering where she fits, who her people are, and how to spend her days.

Truth be told, her confession was freeing to me. It was a reminder that, like so many things in life, belonging is not linear. The trajectory is not straight and upward. Rarely do we arrive. Even the places and faces that feel like perfection do not last forever, but often fade or form into something else. Not always good or bad—just different. Because when it comes to belonging, there is ebb, and there is flow. People come. People go. People change. Sometimes God's presence is so thick we can practically feel his hand upon our shoulders, while other times silence causes us to question whether he was ever really there at all.

For me, the most difficult thing about belonging is that it is neither static nor fully predictable. I have known deep contentment in solitude and the sting of isolation amid a sea of familiar faces. There is no magic number, place, or people that we can attach to our beings like a bandage. Life is in a constant state of flux, and our belonging often rides like a bobber upon the waves. There will be days when we feel inclined not toward celebration, but toward despair. We will find ourselves falling silent as people once safe turn unsteady. We will be tired of always being the one who goes first, the one constantly reaching out with little to no return. We will not only want to cave inward, but to let the brick wall crumble right down on top of us because belonging appears impossible.

Not long ago, I had to step away from a creative community I loved. It was within this community that I had begun to call myself a writer, where I found a group of people who also dreamed of writing books and wrestled with regular bouts of self-doubt, rejection, and the angst that often comes with extending our work and words into the world. The people I found there encouraged and stretched me in the best of ways. I will never diminish the gift that this community was (and is) to me.

But things change. Community cultures shift. Places that once fit begin to feel like a too-tight sweater. And in the fall of 2022, I sensed God's nudge to let go and move on. I knew in my gut it was the right decision. But in the months that followed, I found myself relationally adrift. I was like a boat in the ocean without a paddle, wondering how I would find my way. And while over time my feet eventually found the steadiness of land, in those early moments and days all I could do was borrow hope and celebrate a belonging that was yet to be.

Borrowed Hope

On the night he was arrested, before being taken away, Jesus gathered around the table with his disciples, the faithful friends and followers who had walked with him on dusty roads, felt the residual sting of his rejection, and witnessed the gentle way he drew near the poor and the marginalized. As his hours on earth wound down, he prayed not only for himself and his disciples but also for us—the believers yet to come. He prayed:

> May they all be one, as you, Father, are in me and I am in you. May they also be in us, so that the world may believe you sent me. I have given them the glory you have given me, so that they may be one as we are one. I am in them and you are in me, so that they may be made completely one, that the world may know you have sent me and have loved them as you have loved me.

I return to this prayer often, reminding myself that the way of belonging is not over and Jesus' prayer echoes over us still. His vision remains, even when we are uncertain, unsteady, or very much alone. And like a road map, his prayer can be a place of returning. His words can ground us in who we are and where we have come from, while at the same time turning our shoulders toward the future, inviting us, "Look up! This is not the end. There is so much yet to be."

I hold Jesus' hope when I cannot find my own. I borrow his vision when my eyes feel blind, when I am not inclined toward connection, let alone celebration. I read his words—and then read them again—letting the rhythmic cadence of "I in them and you in me" dance across my shoulders until I begin to sway. Slowly to the left, then to the right, and then back again. The prayer burrows inside me. When I cannot see beyond my situation, his words tip my eyes heavenward until small stars poke through the night sky. I cannot see them clearly, their light still dim and far off. But it is enough. These glimmers of goodness ignite a small spark of gratitude—for the welcome that is here and all that is yet to be.

The Tables to Come

Today there are picnic tables outside the downtown space where I am working. It's spring in Indiana, and the landscape is cloud-covered and dreary. No one is outside. But the tables will not be vacant forever. Soon enough, the weather will warm. The lights strung across the patio will glow against the evening sky, and people will gather. Voices will echo against the brick buildings as the smell of barbecue and beer hang thick in the air. I make a mental note to come back, maybe bring Ben and the boys or some friends over the summer.

Perhaps subconsciously a part of me has always been looking for places to gather, and moments like this are simply a reverberation of that little girl I once was, uninhibited and eager to fill picnic tables end to end. But deep down, I know it is more than that—more than remnants of a past. The desire for communion is still very present, like a plant reaching out toward light that is yet to be.

And goodness, I hope we keep reaching.

Because as human beings in a broken world, not everything will be perfect. Loneliness will still come at us like waves, and our humanity will crash into one another. We will bruise and be bruised, sometimes without even noticing. But there is freedom in knowing we have not yet arrived. We are simply still on our way. Knowing that the eternal table has already been set, we can stand on our tiptoes with expectance, always on the lookout for those first sprouts of hope. We can remember who we are and the belovedness tucked into our tender corners, no longer diminishing the ache for communion grafted into our souls. We can throw our arms wide open to one another in warmth and celebration. Because despite all the ways we get lost, belonging is a welcome we carry with us, setting us free to become people who are held and who hold.

Moving Closer

As we come to the end of the book, consider finding a consistent way to practice celebration. It does not have to be complicated. We do not have to throw elaborate parties or invite all our neighbors over for a barbecue (although that might be fun too!). Celebration can be as simple as paying attention to the places and people around us and calling out the goodness we see in one another. Instead of thinking, *Oh, he's really talented* or *She makes me feel safe*, we can actually tell the person. Maybe we take a little extra effort to commemorate important dates with a gift card or cup of coffee. Again, we do not have to make celebration an elaborate affair. But through a regular habit of calling out good when we see it, we resist the urge to side-eye one another and cultivate relationships based on being seen, known, and appreciated. We plant seeds of hope, watered by a belonging that far extends our own.

Epilogue

A LITURGY FOR WHEN BELONGING FEELS FAR OFF

> Life meanders like a path through the woods.
> We have seasons when we flourish and seasons
> when the leaves fall from us, revealing our bare bones.
> Given time, they grow again.

KATHERINE MAY

The strange thing about writing a book on belonging is the amount of aloneness required to do the work. This season has asked me to live much like a hermit or monk, due to the mental, emotional, and relational capacity book-writing requires. I was often lonely. I felt disconnected. I grew tired of saying no to friends' invitations to grab dinner or catch up and sad when the invitations slowed down. I wanted to reach out to reconnect but knew I was not in a season of pressing in but pulling back, and because of that, the longing was right at the surface of my skin as I penned every word.

This belonging thing is not easy. Sooner or later (if not now), we will wonder once again whether we are really wanted. Self-doubt will rise within us, and like people looking through the glass, we will peer into other's lives like outsiders, filled with desire and desperate to fit in. We will be tempted to strut like peacocks rather than extend our arms in welcome. And as loneliness rises, we will question not only who we are and who God is but also whether communion is really possible on this earth. We will wonder: *Is the way of belonging even worth it?*

In these moments, all I can offer is a simple prayer—a liturgy that we can read together and in private, in our homes and in our churches, in the golden glow of morning and when darkness presses in at night. Like all liturgy, the words are not a prescription or a potion, as if recitation holds some special power. The words are here to keep us grounded while pointing us back to God and one another. It is a common prayer that helps us kneel down in the dirt of our lives and acknowledge that we are people in the middle, and even here, there is hope.

I share it with you as something to hold when belonging seems slippery and a way to remember you are not alone. You are part of a great cloud wandering through the desert, lost and loved human people just trying to make their way Home.

A Liturgy for When Belonging Feels Far Off

Father God, from the very beginning,
you folded your welcome within us like a divine inheritance.
You tucked with-ness into every corner of our personhood,
Unseen and yet firmer than the bones in our bodies.
But many days, the sun sets in bitterness,
and isolation creeps around every corner.
Loneliness presses in like a fog,
And the promise of communion flickers like a distant candle.

God Who Sees, find us even here.
Help us remember who you are
and who you made us to be.
May we not grow jaded by our wanting,
but always reaching out to you and to each other.
Jesus, keep the echoes of your prayer alive when hope is dim,
So that "I in them, you in me" rises like an anthem
And every breath is a reminder we belong.

ACKNOWLEDGMENTS

A book never contains the fingerprints of only one person. And as I sit down to thank all the people who have directly and indirectly touched *The Way of Belonging*, my first acknowledgment is that this space is not enough. But I will do my best to make the most of it.

I want to start by thanking God, but every attempt at expressing the swell of gratitude within me seems to fall short. So I'm going to keep my thanks close, trusting he knows how to translate the swirl into something more sacred and how grateful I am to call him Friend.

Because writing is often very solitary, I am humbled by the generosity of fellow writers who have walked with me over the years. Some of you have graciously reached back a hand to help me find my way when I was googling "What is a book proposal?" while others have faithfully stood beside me in the day to day as I figured out how to move the words from my head to the page. For this book in particular, I want to thank Tasha Jun, Jenai Auman, Sara Billups, Merideth Hite-Estevez, Lore Ferguson Wilbert, and Missy Bari for being my co-laborers. You all kept me going.

And what would a book be without a literary agent and ace publishing team? Still only half-baked in my head. Friends, bringing a book into the world is a wonder, and I would never want to navigate the process alone. I am exceedingly grateful to my literary agent Ingrid Beck at The Bindery, whose steadfast wisdom encouraged me to mature what was once a very infant idea, not to mention all her wizardry with the business side of publishing. Additionally, I could not say enough good things about my editor Cindy Bunch and the rest of the InterVarsity Press team. Every time I got too close to the project and my vision started to blur, they helped me step back and find the thread. From start to finish, their support and guidance has been a gift.

But even before the writing or the publishing, the ideas embedded within *The Way of Belonging* were formed amid relationships. I have been so lucky to have friends who are better at this connection thing than I am and whose very presence has taught me how to embrace and extend welcome in very meaningful, everyday ways. But so many people have influenced these pages that I'm kind of nervous about leaving anyone out (in a book about belonging, no less). So I'm not going to create a long list. But if you and I have had a conversation about community, shared a meal, navigated an existential crisis over Voxer, walked the halls of a college dorm in the middle of the night, or been in a small group or book club anytime over the last decade, thank you. Your hand is in this.

And I'm going to let you in on a secret: it's a weird thing to be married to a person who writes. The details of your life are never fully your own. And while I work really hard to keep the sacred things sacred, Ben has also been very gracious in letting me bring our shared stories to the page. In this way, he loves me well and continues to be my biggest cheerleader, defender, and protector of time and space when words need to be written. He has let me cry and kept me belly laughing, and not a single person would have held this book without him.

I also want to thank our boys (C, T, J, and M) for knowingly (but mostly unknowingly) teaching me so much about the beautiful complexities of being human. Like four flavors of ice cream, each of our boys is distinct, and those differences consistently invite me into a wider way of seeing the world. Plus, they make this wild little life pretty darn sweet.

Last, it doesn't seem right to end without acknowledging Mom, Dad, Laura, Emily, and Michael—the original six whose overlapping stories are peppered throughout this book. Growing up is a strange thing, because even with the same rules and same parents we can experience "home" in such different ways. And despite all the times our humanity has bumped into one another over the years, I am so stinking grateful for how much we still genuinely like each other. Mom and Dad, you done good.

GROUP GUIDE

> Do I want to be not just the one who is being forgiven,
> but also the one who forgives; not just the one
> who is being welcomed home, but also the one
> who welcomes home; not just the one who receives
> compassion, but the one who offers it as well?

HENRI J. M. NOUWEN

The journey of belonging is both inward and outward. It is nestled in the embrace of the Father and in becoming an extension of his welcome. While this guide is designed to facilitate conversations with other people to reorient ourselves to a different way of approaching connection and community, personal reflection must often come first. Many of us need time to unearth and name that which is often buried within us before we can offer an honest response to others.

Therefore, the guide is divided into two parts to mirror the main sections of the book, and within each part, you can find questions for both personal reflection and group discussion. I recommend that you utilize a journal or another note-taking device as you work through the personal reflection questions, both as a physical way to process your responses as well as a way to remember your thoughts once you're together with your group. (Sometimes nerves cause the brain to go blank, at least for me.) Don't rush yourself but set aside at least thirty minutes to an hour to go through the questions.

As you gather together, go gently. The guide is designed for groups to discuss part one and part two separately (ideally in two separate sessions), but you may decide to spread them out or go through all the group questions at once. Your group can decide what pace works best. Whatever you decide, remember that belonging is experienced differently by each of us, and when we gather, we need to make ample space for the narratives of others. Plus, everyone might be a little nervous. Perhaps before you begin, ask God for humility to hear, wisdom to ask good questions, and courage to offer your responses with authenticity while still protecting the sacred pieces of your story. Give yourselves permission to go slowly, and if a question is too deep too soon, by all means, skip it.

A special note to group leaders: people rarely pick up a book or join a group centered on belonging because they have relationships mastered. Many of us come to the topic lonely and acutely aware of our need. Perhaps some people are new to the area or to your group. So before you gather together, spend some time creating a welcoming atmosphere. Consider how well the individuals do or do not know each other, and before diving into the group questions, carve out some space for casual conversation and introductions. Food can always help nervous hands and hearts, so consider beginning your gathering at the table, with a meal or a comforting snack. You can spend that time getting to know details about one another, letting small talk lead into deeper conversation while also remembering that many of us need plenty of runway before getting beneath the surface.

Above all, I hope that by sitting together, sharing space, listening, and (hopefully) enjoying some good snacks, you can begin to see a little more of yourselves in each other. May God meet you in this time and place as you settle further into his welcome.

Part I: Who We Are

Belonging is not dependent on particular places or people. It is not a mold we must pour ourselves into, hoping we will fit. Belonging is a welcome we carry with us. The concept of "you are welcome" is twofold. As a person made in the image of God, you are welcome into the wideness of the Father's embrace, and at the same time, you are welcome to become an extension of that embrace in the world. Welcome is within you. This way of seeing belonging often runs against the current of modern culture, so as you enter into this week's questions, take some time to consider how reframing the ways you think of yourself, of God, and of each other might impact your sense of connectedness in your day-to-day life.

Read: Chapters 1–5

Personal Reflection

- Think about a time you felt out of place. What happened? Who was there? What were you thinking? Feeling? How did you respond?

- How did your early experiences shape how you relate to God and other people? As you look back, do any key moments, specific stories, or wounds stand out?

- The instinct to hide is human. (We've been doing it since the beginning.) Are there parts of yourself that you try to keep hidden from God or other people?

- When you think about the welcome of God that is not only offered to you but is within you, do you have any underlying fears, concerns, doubts, or questions? Write them down or say them out loud, as a prayer.

Group Discussion

- Looking back at your personal reading and reflection, do you have any thoughts, questions, or comments you'd like to share?

- What quotes, stories, or ideas stood out to you in these chapters?

- Based on what you've read, how would you define "the way of belonging"?

- How does the book's description of belonging differ from your previously held definitions?

- In Jesus' story of the lost sons (Luke 15:11-32), do you relate to the lostness of one son more than the other? Or perhaps both? Feel free to share why, if you are comfortable.

- Growing up, what was your image of God?

- In what ways has that picture changed or remained the same?

- Have you ever felt like you had to change or hide who you are in order to be part of a group? If so, how?

- Describe places or people who have felt like home. What were the qualities of those spaces that made you feel welcomed?

- In what ways do you sense God inviting you to approach belonging in a different way?
- What would you like to take with you from these chapters or our conversation?

Part II: How We Relate

Belonging invites us to be who we are while becoming the love of the Father. He invites us to be an extension of his embrace. While we cannot find a prescription or five-step program to manufacture belonging, we can cultivate postures and practices that help us walk a way of welcome. The postures and practices go hand in hand, and one may be more essential in certain seasons. The point is not perfection but journeying together as we look inward, move closer, and allow God's love to change how we relate, right in the middle of our everyday lives.

Read: Chapters 6–16

Personal Reflection

- What does your ache to belong tell you about God and the way your humanity is wired?
- What are some of the lack narratives you carry into relationships? (Ex: "I am not good enough" or "If I'm too this or that, they will leave" or "I am not really a people person.")
- In what ways do you gravitate toward people who are the same or different from yourself?
- Do you ever feel pressure to have answers or be an expert? If so, why do you think that is?
- What keeps you from wading deeper into relationships?

- Do you tend to approach relationships from a lens of scarcity or abundance?

- Is there a particular posture or practice you want to lean into in this next season?

Group Discussion

- Look back at your personal reading and reflections. Do you have any thoughts, questions, or comments you'd like to share?

- What stories, quotes, or ideas stood out to you in these chapters?

- By default, do you tend to view your desire to belong as lack or longing? A personal deficiency or God-given design?

- How does reframing lack as longing change how you view your desire to belong?

- Have you ever misread a person or a situation?

- In what ways does getting to know a person's story impact how you relate to them?

- Do you ever feel pressure (internally or externally) to have answers or be an expert?

- How comfortable are you with saying your questions out loud to others?

- Do you tend to dive into the deep end of relationships too quickly? Or are you naturally more hesitant to wade deeper into connection?

- Has anyone modeled generativity to you, either personally or professionally?

- How might the practice of celebration help counteract the tendency toward consumerism and grasping?

- Is there a posture or practice that you'd like to continue working into your daily rhythms?

- What would you like to take with you from these chapters or our conversation?

Endings can be awkward. As you wrap up reading this book together, I suggest that you turn to the epilogue and read "A Liturgy for When Belonging Feels Far Off" out loud with one another. Again, the prayer is not magic, but perhaps it can be a good way to mark the moment and move forward together.

NOTES

Foreword

ix *The psychiatrist Curt Thompson*: Curt Thompson (@curt_thompsonmd), Twitter/X, January 18, 2022, https://twitter.com/curt_thompsonmd/status /1483409010351120389?lang=en.

1. Out of Place

11 *"To be human"*: Ryan Kuja, interview by Sarah E. Westfall, *Not My Story* podcast (Episode 36), June 9, 2021.

3. The God Who Finds Us

27 *"What brought the father joy"*: About a year after losing our second-born son Carter, I read Skye Jethani's book *With: Reimagining the Way You Relate to God* (Nashville, TN: Thomas Nelson, 2011) along with some friends, and the entire experience was deeply formative. It helped me more clearly see the communal nature of God and gave me permission not to try so stinking hard. *With* has become my most-recommended book for anyone who is trying to untangle a performance-based spirituality.

4. Everything Is Yours

39 *"Be still"*: This quote is from Psalm 46, which became a place of soothing during those raw days of grief.

40 *"You are good"*: This reference is a callback both to the creation narrative of Genesis 2 as well as Psalm 139, which describes the far-reaching ways in which God knows and loves us.

"farther up and further in": C. S. Lewis, *The Last Battle* (New York: Harper-Collins, 2000).

41 *"Becoming like the heavenly Father"*: Henri J. M. Nouwen, *The Return of the Prodigal Son: A Story of Homecoming* (New York: Doubleday, 1992), 125.

42 *Love, joy, peace*: In Galatians 5:22-23, Paul refers to these qualities as the "fruit of the Spirit," indicators of a deeply formed life in Christ.

5. A Mobile Home

45 *The word* belong: *Online Etymology Dictionary*, s.v. "belong," accessed May 24, 2023, www.etymonline.com/word/belong.

belong *is a verb*: *Chambers Dictionary of Etymology* (New York: Chambers Harrap Publishers, 1988), s.v. "belong," 88.

45 *"Why pay so much attention"*: Henri J. M. Nouwen, *The Return of the Prodigal Son: A Story of Homecoming* (New York: Doubleday, 1992).

46 *You discover the fullness*: When pressed, Jesus told the Pharisees that all the Scriptures (the Law and the Prophets) could be distilled into one command, "love the Lord," and the second, "love your neighbor," was not far from it. You can find this conversation in Matthew 22:37-39.

47 *walk each other Home*: The phrase "walking each other home" is a phrase popularized by Ram Dass, and while I do not know or necessarily ascribe to all his philosophies, I find this phrase to be a beautiful image of what belonging looks like in the world as we stand amid both the earthly and the eternal.

48 *"shake the dust"*: Three of the four Gospels (Matthew 10:14; Mark 6:11; Luke 9:5) cite this quote from Jesus, where he urged his disciples to leave a place where they are not welcomed with their peace intact.

6. From Lack to Longing

60 *Abraham Maslow's hierarchy*: Maslow's hierarchy of needs is helpful in understanding the various categories of need that are common to our humanity. However, Maslow tended to elevate the physical needs over the relational or emotional needs in terms of importance, and I would contend that all contain equal weight when it comes to pursuing health and wholeness.

"take this cup": In Mark 14:32-42, right before he was arrested, Jesus went into the Garden of Gethsemane and expressed how he longed for a different way. Eventually, he surrendered to the cross and days of death that were to come, and while his longing did not change his circumstance, his prayers led him to the Father and armed him with courage nonetheless.

61 *"Desire is the very substance"*: Curt Thompson, *The Soul of Desire* (Downers Grove, IL: InterVarsity Press, 2021), 25.

62 *eternity embedded in our hearts*: The phrase "eternity embedded in our hearts" is a reference to Ecclesiastes 3:11, which says, "He has made everything appropriate in its time. He has also put eternity in their hearts."

7. The Art of Naming

65 *Whether my outsider status*: The idea that feeling out of place can sometimes be imagined or internalized came from a conversation with Emily P. Freeman. You can find the original conversation here: Sarah E. Westfall (sarah_westfall), "I have not found all the words," Instagram, August 25, 2022, www.instagram.com/p/ChsISUugf7q/?utm_source=ig_web_copy_link.

66 *"see what he would call it"*: You can find the full narrative in Genesis 2.

67 *"What are you looking for?"*: In his book *The Soul of Desire* (Downers Grove, IL: InterVarsity Press, 2021), Dr. Curt Thompson really digs into this

question from a theological, physiological, and psychological framework. It was a conversation with Curt on the *Not My Story* podcast that first directed my attention to this question, so it feels important to mention here, both for transparency and as an additional resource.

72   *"in the ancient world"*: John H. Walton, Victor H. Matthews, and Mark W. Chavalas, *The IVP Bible Background Commentary: Old Testament* (Downers Grove, IL: InterVarsity Press, 2000), 29.

"it contained the deity's essence": Walton, Matthews, and Chavalas, *IVP Bible Background Commentary*, 29.

8. From Them to Us

80   *"our ability to silo ourselves"*: Geoffrey L. Cohen, *Belonging: The Science of Creating Connection and Bridging Divides* (New York: W. W. Norton, 2022).

what seems "other": Author Jenai Auman often uses the word *othered* to refer to individuals who have been pressed to the fringes, overlooked, or out of place. I borrow her use of the word here, noting that there are many ways to be othered.

81   *When we embed our identity*: In *Belonging: The Science of Creating Connection and Bridging Divides*, Cohen writes that being part of a group—even a hate group—can bolster one's sense of significance, where acts on behalf of the "we" (even if they are harmful to another person) elicit feelings of meaning and worth, even if it means we have to shrink ourselves or hide a little of who we are to be in the group.

82   *"we who are many"*: The passage I quote here is from Romans 12:3-8, but you can find other similar teachings in 1 Corinthians 12 and Ephesians 4.

83   *Unity is not uniformity*: On *The Holy Post* podcast (Ep. 501, March 23, 2022), Gabriel Salguero said, "We need unity, not uniformity." This quote stuck with me.

9. The Stories Between Us

91   *"Human minds yield"*: Jonathan Gottschall, *The Storytelling Animal: How Stories Make Us Human* (Boston: Houghton Mifflin Harcourt, 2012).

92   *fundamental attribution error*: Geoffrey L. Cohen, *Belonging: The Science of Creating Connection and Bridging Divides* (New York: W. W. Norton, 2022).

basic principle of FAE: Cohen, *Belonging*.

Our snap reactions: Cohen, *Belonging*.

93   *"leaves little room"*: Cohen, *Belonging*.

94   *"When a person tells her story"*: Curt Thompson, *Anatomy of the Soul: Surprising Connections Between Neuroscience and Spiritual Practices That Can Transform Your Life and Relationships* (Carol Stream, IL: Tyndale Momentum, 2010).

95 *story allows us to peek through*: In *Walden* (Barnes & Noble, 2003), Henry David Thoreau asks, "Could a greater miracle take place than for us to look through each other's eyes for an instant?"

96 *"complexities and contradictions"*: Cohen, *Belonging*.

10. From Certain to Settled

100 *"generally accepting and responsive"*: APA Dictionary of Psychology, s.v. "secure attachment," accessed April 26, 2023, https://dictionary.apa .org/secure-attachment.

"virtually every action": Curt Thompson, *Anatomy of the Soul: Surprising Connections Between Neuroscience and Spiritual Practices That Can Transform Your Life and Relationships* (Carol Stream, IL: Tyndale House, 2010), 109.

101 *Perfectly situated*: Mark Cartwright, s.v. "Thessalonica," WorldHistory.org (May 1, 2016), accessed August 2022, www.worldhistory.org/Thessalonica.

103 *"It's all essential"*: John Blase, interviewed by Sarah E. Westfall on *Not My Story* podcast (Episode 3), May 5, 2021.

we are like waves: James K. A. Smith, *How to Inhabit Time: Understanding the Past, Facing the Future, Living Faithfully Now* (Grand Rapids, MI: Brazos Press, 2022).

people of humus: *Chambers Dictionary of Etymology* (New York: Chambers Harrap Publishers, 1988), s.v.v. "humble" and "humus," 496.

104 *"True, authentic humility"*: Daryl Van Tongeren, *Humble: Free Yourself from the Traps of a Narcistic World* (New York: The Experiment, 2022).

"Humility is a way": Tongeren, *Humble*.

105 *"Community exposes"*: "How We Change: Community" was a sermon by pastor and author John Mark Comer, the audio of which can now be found at practicingtheway.org. The entire message is worth a listen.

106 *"the kingdoms of the world"*: This quote comes from Matthew 4, a passage that retells the time when Jesus is led by the Spirit into the wilderness for forty days and experiences a series of temptations. This wilderness experience seemed to be a measure of preparation for Jesus as he launched a more public life, and one of the first things Jesus did after that event is to ask the brothers Peter and Andrew to follow him.

11. Say the Questions

108 *Formerly St. Anthony Novitiate*: Dan Kurtz, "Lakewood Park Church Marks 60 Years," KPCNews, October 23, 2010, www.kpcnews.com/article_6218 ac55-4940-52bf-8a21-11decb6b8936.html.

110 *"live the questions"*: Rainer Maria Rilke, *Letters to a Young Poet* (New York: Penguin Random House, 2014).

111 *"God created you curious"*: Lore Wilbert, *A Curious Faith: The Questions God Asks, We Ask, and We Wish Someone Would Ask Us* (Grand Rapids, MI: Brazos Press, 2022), 58.

112 *The moment we think*: Daryl Van Tongeren, *Humble: Free Yourself from the Traps of a Narcistic World* (New York: The Experiment, 2022).

12. From Breadth to Depth

126 *"Lord, make me a channel"*: "Mother Teresa Acceptance Speech," The Nobel Prize, accessed April 4, 2023, www.nobelprize.org/prizes/peace/1979/teresa/acceptance-speech.

127 *"If we really believe"*: "Mother Teresa Acceptance Speech."

"first in our own home": "Mother Teresa Acceptance Speech."

13. Circles of Belonging

132 *"We need others to bear witness"*: Curt Thompson, *The Soul of Desire: Discovering the Neuroscience of Longing, Beauty, and Community* (Downers Grove, IL: InterVarsity Press, 2021), 98-99.

134 *"true belonging"*: Brené Brown, *Braving the Wilderness: The Quest for True Belonging and the Courage to Stand Alone* (New York: Random House, 2017), 40.

136 *the tabernacle was considered the* Mishkan: *Encyclopaedia Britannica*, s.v. "Tabernacle," updated November 2, 2023, www.britannica.com/topic/Tabernacle.

136 *Only the high priest*: *Encyclopaedia Britannica*, s.v. "Holy of Holies," updated October 24, 2023, www.britannica.com/topic/Holy-of-Holies.

137 *"we are created in and for community"*: Parker Palmer, *Let Your Life Speak: Listening for the Voice of Vocation* (San Francisco: Jossey-Bass, 2000), 49.

139 *circles of belonging*: I amended this practice from a psychological theory called Dunbar's number, which outlines how many people any human can really connect with at any given moment. This theory breaks these relationships (ranging from loved ones to people you can recognize on the street) into concentric circles. While I do not hold strictly to the number he proposes to allow for our unique relational capacity, I do want to give credit to this idea of "circles" of increased transparency to British anthropologist Robin Dunbar. ("Dunbar's number: Why we can only maintain 150 relationships," *BBC*, accessed August 24, 2023, at bbc.com/future/article/20191001-dunbars-number-why-we-can-only-maintain-150-relationships.)

14. From Consume to Create

144 *Consumerism is so embedded*: My thoughts in this section were shaped in part by Tim Suttle's book *Shrink: Faithful Ministry in a Church-Growth*

Culture (Grand Rapids, MI: Zondervan, 2014). It's a hard but good read about how this consumerist mindset has infiltrated the American church.

144   *Matthew Perry's memoir*: Matthew Perry, *Friends, Lovers, and the Big Terrible Thing: A Memoir* (New York: Flatiron Books, 2022).

145   *He postured himself as a creator*: I want to add a personal note here acknowledging the grief I felt in Matthew Perry's passing in 2023, roughly six months after I wrote these words. It's strange when you know people only from a distance, and yet in some way, they're important to you. Perry was one of those people for me. I am grateful for his life, and I grieve his death.

     "We are Imago Dei*"*: Makoto Fujimura, *Art and Faith: A Theology of Making* (New Haven, CT: Yale University Press, 2020).

146   *"by allowing something to die"*: Parker Palmer, *Let Your Life Speak: Listening for the Voice of Vocation* (San Francisco: Jossey-Bass, 2000), 91.

147   *"I glance around the pews"*: Ben Palpant, *Letters from the Mountain* (Nashville, TN: Rabbit Room Press, 2021).

     The posture is not "look at me": I have heard Emily P. Freeman talk many times about "building benches, not platforms" in relation to our work as writers, but I think the concept holds value in all our relationships.

149   *"the journey of loving"*: This phrase came from a conversation writer Helena Sorensen had with Matt Conner on episode two of the *Call It Good* podcast (April 28, 2022). You can find the official transcript by visiting https://rabbitroom.com/call-it-good-transcripts/.

150   *not by fame but by faithfulness*: This concept of faithfulness (not success) being a marker of the people of God comes from Tim Suttle in his book *Shrink*.

     "Artists have always been drawn": Madeleine L'Engle, *Walking on Water: Reflections on Faith & Art* (New York: Convergent Books, 2016), 153.

151   *trying to eliminate vices*: We attended College Wesleyan Church in Marion, Indiana, from roughly 2006–2012, and these thoughts on vice and virtue came from a sermon by Steve DeNeff, who was lead teaching pastor at that time.

15. Seeds of Confetti

161   *"May they all be one"*: This portion of Jesus' prayer is from verses 21-23 (CSB), but you can find the entire prayers for all believers in John 17:20-26.